Axolotls, Mexican Salamanders as Pets.

Axolotl care, facts, diet, aquarium, habitat, breeding, diseases and where to buy all included.

The Axolotl Complete Owner's Guide.

by

Elliott Lang

## *Table of Contents*

# Table of Contents

# *Chapter 1. Introduction*

The very first axolotl that I received had been a surprise. I knew that I had wanted to add a salamander or newt into my collection of unusual pets but I hadn't narrowed down the search to the axolotl itself.

Actually, my first instinct was to choose a salamander of one kind or another. During my research, I stumbled across the world of  the axolotl and instantly fell in love with this unique and playful little creature.

After spending a lot of time researching, I set up my tank, or rather tanks, and I ventured out into the world to purchase my first axolotl. Finding a breeder was a bit challenging but after looking everywhere, I found one I felt comfortable with and it wasn't long before my axolotl was safely in his home.

That being said, purchasing and owning an axolotl has changed greatly over the years since my first axolotl. For one, more and more people are realizing how truly remarkable this species is. This means that the axolotl is easier to find, since more breeders have appeared on the scene.

For two, the world wide web has made finding a breeder much easier to do.

However, that being said, one of the largest problems with axolotls today is the lack of information on them. While it is easier to find a young or adult axolotl, it is next to impossible to find the actual information you need for its care.

That is where the inspiration for this book came from. Not only did I realize that I had a wealth of information on axolotl but I could offer it to other people.

This book has been designed with the amateur axolotl enthusiast in mind but it can be an excellent resource for the experienced breeder.

It starts off by looking at the axolotl in a quick snapshot. From there, I take you through everything you need to know about axolotls, from their personality to their anatomy.

Once you have a firm understanding of what an axolotl is, I look at everything you need to know about your axolotl's care. I go over everything, including the best types of habitats, feeding your axolotl and what to expect from the axolotl in your tank.

In addition, I will go over breeding your axolotl and how to determine the sex of your animal. This is a comprehensive guide that will give you all the information you need to have an aquarium that will showcase and sustain your axolotl.

I know, personally, that an axolotl can be an amazing addition to your aquarium and they really don't need a lot of extras in regards to care. Still, there are a few things that you should do to make sure your axolotl is healthy and stays that way.

That is really what this book is all about. Bringing you the wonder of the axolotl, while giving you all the important information on how to properly care for him.

# Chapter 2. The Interesting Axolotl

Let me introduce you to the axolotl, which is an aquatic amphibian that has begun to gain popularity as a household pet. It is an interesting animal that is full of many personality traits and interesting characteristics. To  name a few, the axolotl retains its larval stage throughout its life and it has the ability to regenerate limbs and other body parts.

It is a pet that is actually quite easy to care for and the axolotl is wonderful for enthusiasts of all ages.

In this chapter, I will go over a variety of facts about axolotl and will discuss exactly what an axolotl is.

## 1. What is the Axolotl?

The axolotl is an interesting animal that is native to Michocacan, Mexico. It is actually a salamander that retains its larvae state throughout its life, which is known as neoteny.

Also known as the Mexican Salamander or water monster, it is often mistaken for other species, such as the Mexican Tiger Salamander or the water dog. Although this mistake is often made, the Axolotl is actually a species of its own that is endangered in its wild habitat.

In captivity, however, it is thriving and more people are becoming besotted with this playful animal. The axolotl's name comes from Nahuatl, which is a form of the Aztec language. It is believed to have been linked to the Mexican god, Xolotl, who is the god of deformation and death, in Aztec mythology.

The axolotl, itself, is an interesting animal that retains its larval appearance throughout its life and does not lose its gills or fins as an adult. In addition, the axolotl reaches sexual maturity in its larval state and does not need to undergo the metamorphosis into a salamander to breed.

Although it is an amphibian, the axolotl does not live outside of water. In fact, it is completely aquatic and while it can survive out of water for short periods, it should never be housed in an aquarium that does not have deep water.

## *2. History of Axolotl*

The Axolotl has a long history and no one knows when it evolved in the wild. What we do know is that the axolotl is an anomaly in the role of evolution. In fact, it is believed that the axolotl is a step back in evolution from another salamander species that went through the metamorphosis from the larvae stage to the amphibian.

Another interesting fact about the history of the axolotl is that this evolution only took place in one area of the world. In fact, it only took place in one location and that was in Michocacan, Mexico.

The axolotl is native to only two lakes in that state – Lake Xochimilco and Lake Chalco and its natural habitat is being put in danger from the ever expanding Mexico City.

As a result of this, and the fact that the axolotl is sold as meat in Mexico, the axolotl is quickly disappearing from its natural habitat. There is believed to be an estimated 1200 adult axolotl in the wild. This revelation has led to the axolotl being placed on the endangered species list.

Despite the decreasing numbers in the wild, captive bred and raised axolotl are doing well. They were first brought into captivity in 1863 when six adult axolotls were shipped to Jardin des Plantes in Paris. It was at this time that Auguste Dumeril discovered that the axolotl did not mature into a salamander but instead, kept their larvae form in a state of neoteny.

From these first 6 axolotl, research began on both neoteny and regeneration, since the axolotl is surprisingly adept at regenerating limbs and other parts of its body.

In fact, it is its ability to regrow limbs that has seen its population swell in captivity. They have proven extremely easy to breed in captivity and axolotl have thrived in this setting.

Today, they are still used in research facilities in an attempt to unlock the secrets behind cell regeneration. From these captive, research axolotl, the pet population began to take off and today, more and more people are enjoying their very own axolotl.

## 3. General Facts about the Axolotl

Before you decide on getting an axolotl, it is important to know a few of the general facts about them. While I go over everything you need to know about axolotl throughout this book, the general facts of the axolotl will serve as a snapshot to give you a better idea of whether this is a pet for you or not.

### Do axolotl make good pets?

Yes, axolotl make excellent pets and are very interesting to watch and interact with. They can be trained to take food from your hand and they will often become excited when you see you.

They are not a pet that you can handle, however, and they must stay in their aquarium. So if you are looking for a pet that you can train, walk and pet, then the axolotl is not the right pet for you. If you are looking for a pet to enjoy watching, like you would with fish, then the axolotl can be a wonderful pet to have.

### Are they a good pet for children to have?

Since axolotl are fairly easy to care for, they can be a wonderful pet for children. That being said, this is not a pet that a child can hold and they can often become bored with them. In addition, the cleaning of the tank must be done by an adult, as the process can be quite complex.

If you have an older child who enjoys watching fish, then the axolotl is a great aquarium amphibian for them. However, if the child prefers to tap on the glass or place things in the tank, which the axolotl could swallow, then this isn't a pet for them.

### Are they clean?

In general terms, axolotl are very clean animals, as they are confined to one aquarium. However, when it comes to cleanliness in the aquarium, axolotl are quite messy.

Seeing as they eat live food, they often leave decaying flesh in their tanks. This means that you will need to clean it frequently. Light cleaning of the tank has to be done on a weekly basis and a thorough cleaning has to be done once a month.

### *Can they live in any aquarium?*

Yes. In fact, axolotl have even done well living in buckets, although I would not recommend it for a long-term home. The ideal set up for the axolotl is a tank that has a proper filtration system and good water quality. They do need a freshwater system so they are not recommended for any tank that has salt water in it.

### *Do they really regenerate?*

Yes, axolotl do regenerate and this is one of the most interesting traits of the axolotl. If one damages a limb, tail or even an eye, it will grow it back within a matter of months. In addition, occasionally an axolotl will grow an additional limb, even if it has all four.

### *Do you need special equipment for axolotl?*

In regards to equipment, you don't really need anything different for your axolotl than what you would get for any fish. You will need a heater, filters, a good sized aquarium and all of the other equipment necessary for setting up an aquarium. Read the chapter on setting up your aquarium to learn more about the equipment that you need.

### *Are they good for someone new to amphibians?*

If you are looking for an easy pet to care for, then the axolotl is one of them. They do not require a lot of knowledge to care for and this makes them perfect for first time amphibian owners.

### *What is the lifespan of an axolotl?*

Surprisingly, the axolotl has a very long lifespan so anyone interested in adding one to their home should be aware of this. The axolotl can live, on average, 8 to 10 years with many living up to 15 years. Remember, with such a long lifespan, you are making a big commitment to your pet.

### *Are there different types of axolotl?*

No, there are not different types of axolotl, although there have

been some hybrids between two species being sold as axolotl. That being said, there are actually several different colours of axolotl that you can find. Read the chapter on axolotl anatomy for more information on the different colours you can find.

### *How long do they take to mature?*

One of the most interesting facts about axolotl is that they mature while still maintaining their juvenile form. Unlike other salamanders, axolotl maintain their gills throughout their life, even in maturity.

However, the maturity rate for axolotl differs between each individual. Some axolotl can mature as young as 7 months but most mature around 18 to 24 months of age.

### How big do axolotl get?

Axolotl range in size with females often being slightly smaller than males. They tend to range from 8 inches in length to 12 inches in length when they have reached full maturity. Some may be slightly larger or smaller, depending on the quality of care they received during growth; however, this is usually a rare occurrence.

# *Chapter 3. Anatomy of an Axolotl*

Now that you know the general facts and history of the axolotl, I would like to take the time to go over the anatomy of an axolotl. These are truly amazing creatures, as they have the unique trait of retaining their juvenile stage throughout their life, even through their sexual maturity. This is known as neoteny and only a handful of animals on the planet are like this.

The axolotl are one of these animals and it can be a complete pleasure to own an axolotl. In addition to maintaining their juvenile form, the axolotl can regenerate their limbs and other body parts when they are injured.

In this chapter, I will discuss the different parts of axolotl anatomy. Understanding the anatomy will help you in selecting your first axolotl. In addition, it will help you understand your axolotl and know when it is not doing well in an environment.

Finally, at the end of this chapter, I will go over the differences between male and female axolotl and how you can determine it yourself.

## *1. Axolotl Anatomy*

When we look at the basic anatomy of an axolotl, we are actually looking at the juvenile stage of a salamander. This is actually a very interesting fact about the axolotl and what makes it such a wonderful and weird pet.

The axolotl is a predator. It has developed to be carnivorous and for this reason, it will hunt anything that you put in its tank, including fingers if it can get at them. While this can seem scary, the axolotl is peculiar in the fact that its teeth are not those of a predator. In fact, they are actually pedicalate, which means that they are not used for cutting and biting.

In fact, the teeth, which are shaped like small, cone like stumps, are designed for gripping the food and aid in swallowing food whole. The teeth are found on both the upper and lower jaw.

The mouth itself is quite large and it uses a sucking mechanism to suck up food that is close at hand. For this reason, it is imperative that you do not keep any object in the tank that is smaller than the axolotl's head. They will suck it up and this will create blockages in their digestive system.

The axolotl is a poikilothermic animal. What this means is that the axolotl is heated and cooled by its surroundings. Water that is too cold will cause the metabolism of the axolotl to slow down. Water that is too warm will cause the metabolism to speed up.

The skin of the axolotl is very thin and delicate. It can be damaged quite easily so it is important to handle the axolotl with care.

The actual anatomy of the axolotl is very amphibian in nature. It has a three-chambered heart like all amphibians. The main

17

difference is that while amphibians develop function lungs, axolotl maintain rudimentary lungs that do not allow it to live out of water for long periods.

The animal has 50 vertebrae and while they can grow up to 12 inches in length, 70% of that length is their tail. While they are usually a slow moving animal, they can move quite quickly when necessary.

### a) Breathing

Despite the fact that the gills are a very noticeable part of the anatomy, I wanted to discuss them in a separate section, rather than in the actual anatomy section.

First, axolotl retain their gills throughout their life. These gills are large, branch like structures that branch off from their head. They have three gills on either side with fluffy membranes that branch off from the main stem. Their gills are called rami and they are full of capillaries, which are known as fimbrea.

The gills function in the same way as they do with fish. They pull water through the membranes where the capillaries pull the oxygen out of the water and into the body. Co2 is passed back into the water through the gills as well.

One thing to note is that the axolotl does not have to be moving to make his gills work. All he needs to do is move the gills themselves, which means that you will find your axolotl staying still quite often.

When the axolotl are young, gills are often damaged by other axolotl in the tank. In addition, when you purchase an older axolotl from a pet store or breeder, you could end up with damaged gills. Thankfully, damage to the gills does not impede breathing and they regenerate quite quickly.

While most people think that breathing is done through the very decorative gills, axolotl actually breathe in four different methods. The first is through the gills as described above.

In addition to the gills, axolotl will breathe through a method known as cutaneous respiration. This is the process of breathing through the skin.

Basically, this breathing is done when the axolotl moves or when there is a current in the water. The skin of the axolotl is very thin and this allows the oxygen in the water to pass through it easily. Once it passes through the skin, it can be utilized by the body.

The third way that an axolotl breathes is through a method known as buccal respiration.

This form of breathing utilizes the buccopharyngeal membrane, which is a flap of skin near the back of the throat, to absorb oxygen. It works in the same manner as the skin. When water passes over the buccopharyngeal membrane, the oxygen is filtered out of the water.

It should be noted that the buccopharyngeal membrane is very important for the axolotl to eat. When the axolotl sucks in food, it also sucks in water. The buccopharngeal membrane is pushed down and up to suck and push out water that enters into the mouth when eating.

The final way that axolotls breathe is through their very primitive lungs. Remember that they do have lungs, although they are rudimentary. They are strong enough to breath air but not strong enough to be the sole source of breathing for the axolotl.

That being said, axolotls will, from time to time, swim up to the top of the tank and swallow a bubble of air. This bubble causes them to float on the surface of the water but they will burp it out eventually. It is not a common form of breathing for the axolotl but it does offer another way for the axolotl to get oxygen, and it is often very entertaining to watch.

### b) Regeneration

As you know, regeneration is one of the most interesting qualities of the axolotl and is one of the reasons why many people are interested in the species.

In research labs, axolotls are used in an effort to unlock the mysteries behind regeneration. These labs have found that axolotls will regenerate any part of their body and have even successfully accepted

20

transplants, including partial brain transplants, from other axolotls.

Regeneration rate differs depending on the age of the animal, the care it is receiving and also on the temperature of the water. Although it is unclear why, axolotls that are kept in cooler water regenerate faster than those kept in warmer tanks.

At this time, studies have found that axolotl can regenerate any part of their body. They have been known to regenerate limbs, tail, gills, parts of both their peripheral nervous system and central nervous system, heart, kidney tissue, skin tissue, eyes and their liver. They are truly an amazing animal.

Regeneration time varies as I have said. However, in younger animals, a limb can be regenerated within a month. Older adults can take up to six months to regenerate a limb and some lose their ability to regenerate a limb, being unable to regrow one after losing it.

Although it is very interesting to see a limb regenerate, it is imperative that you do not injure the animal on purpose. Regeneration does stress the system of the axolotl and stress can lead to disease.

### c) Slime

The final part of anatomy that I want to look at is the fact that axolotls have a thin slime that covers their body. This slime is very important in protecting the skin of the axolotl and keeping it moist. If you find that your axolotl is dry, then there is a problem and you should get him checked immediately.

## 2. Colouring

When it comes to colouring, you can really find a lot of different choices out there. Trust me, it isn't all just one colour and this is one of the reasons why axolotls can be a wonderful addition to an aquarium. It is also the reason why many people want to have more than one axolotl.

With colouring, there are 6 different colours that you can find in the axolotl. It is important to note that patterns on the skin will vary slightly from animal to animal but below are the colours that you will see.

### *1. Wild Type*

Wild type is the most common type of colouring that is seen and it is the colour that you would see on axolotls that are bred in the wild. Often, wild types have a dark brown colouring to them, but this is a varied colouring.

In fact, there is a large range of colours in the wild type axolotls and they can range from light brown to a dark, almost black, brown.

With the wild type coloration, you will see speckles on the body that are black and yellow, again, shade will range. In addition, the belly of the wild type axolotl is lighter than the top half and the toes will become pale in sexually mature adults.

### *2. Albino*

Albino is an animal that has no pigments in its skin and has no coloration on the skin. It is usually a white coloration, however, some albinos, depending on the parents, may have a cream collared pigmentation and others may have slightly yellowish shading on the body.

Albinos have red eyes as the lack of pigmentation in the eyes allows the red blood vessels to show through. In addition, the gills are usually a vibrant pink coloration, which you do not see in the wild type colour.

Lastly, the toes of an albino will become slightly gray when he is sexually mature.

### 3. Golden Albino

A golden albino sounds like exactly what it is, an albino that has a slightly golden shade to its skin. Like the albino, the eyes of the golden albino are red or pink due to the blood vessels showing through the eye.

The gills are usually a vibrant pink or red coloration, which you do not see in the wild type colour, but the colour is not usually as vibrant as what you would see in an albino.

Lastly, the toes of a golden albino will become slightly gray when he is sexually mature.

### 4. Melanoid

Where albinos lack skin pigmentation, melanoids lack iridophores, which are the shiny patches on the body and around the eyes of an axolotl. What this means is that the melanoid is a very dark axolotl that has a black, or close to black, coloration.

Often, melanoids are mistaken for wild types; however, they can be differentiated by the lack of a shiny ring around the pupil.

Again, the underside of the melanoid may be slightly lighter than the topside and the toes will become pale when the melanoid is sexually mature.

## 5. Leucistic

The leucistic axolotl is an interesting axolotl as it is commonly

mistaken for the albino. It is not actually an albino, even though it does have white skin. Instead of lacking pigmentation, the leucistic has a reduced amount of pigmentation in the body. This creates the white colour.

As there is pigmentation, leucistics can have speckles of black on their body. When the speckles are present, they are known as a piebald leucistic.

In addition to the white skin coloration, leucistic do have red in their eyes, however, it is always surrounded by a ring of black coloration. This is one of the easiest ways to determine the difference between the leucistic and the albino since the albino will have only red in its eyes.

Like the albino, the leucistic will have the pink coloration on the gills; however, it is often a muted shade of pink. Finally, as with all lightly collared axolotl, the toes will become greyish in color when the axolotl is sexually mature.

## 6. Copper

The final colour that you can see in axolotls is the copper colour. This is an interesting color, as it still seems to be fairly uncommon. It is actually more prevalent in Australia than any other country.

Copper axolotls are very similar to wild types when it comes to colouring; however, they are a form of albino axolotl. They have a caramel colour that can range in shade from a very light tan to a dark copper.

The eyes of the copper axolotl are red in colouring, although it is often difficult to see. In addition to the colouring on the skin, there is often some light speckling of a greyish black. The gills are the same colouring as the skin. Finally, the toes of the copper axolotl will become pale when the axolotl has reached sexual maturity.

## 3. Lifecycle of the Axolotl

Seeing as we are looking at an amphibian, it is important to look at the lifecycle of the axolotl for a better understanding of the species. While many owners will not have to worry about the egg and larval stage of the axolotl, if you plan on breeding, which is discussed later in this book, you will want to understand the lifecycle.

To begin, axolotl, like all amphibians, start as an egg that is laid in water and surrounded by a thick, protective jelly. Female axolotls can lay between a 100 to 1000 eggs every time she produces a clutch of eggs. This means that an axolotl can start with a very large family.

The egg itself is very normal when it comes to amphibian eggs. It begins as a single egg, roughly 2mm in diameter, which is surrounded by jelly. The jelly, itself, is made of water and it is used to stabilize the egg and protect it.

The egg takes 2 to 3 weeks to hatch and during that time, the larvae begin to grow and move. It is very interesting watching axolotl eggs develop, as you can see the axolotl quite clearly through the jelly. In the beginning stages, you will need a magnifying glass to see the axolotl, however, closer to hatching time; you will be able to see the axolotl with the naked eye.

After the 3 weeks have passed, the axolotl will hatch out of the jelly. At this stage, the axolotl will look like a small tadpole, without any limbs, and will be about 11mm in size. Some can be larger or smaller, but the majority of your axolotl will be 11mms.

Axolotl larvae are competent hunters and they will be extremely hungry during those first few weeks. In addition, after they hatch, the axolotls will be transparent and this can make watching them even more enjoyable. Not only will you be able to see their lungs, heart and kidneys, but you will also be able to see the progression of food through their digestive tract.

After a few weeks, the axolotl larva will mature enough to have pigmentation in their skin so you shouldn't be able to see through them as easily as before, if at all. In addition, by two weeks of age, the larva will enter into the next stage of development when their legs begin to form.

Although axolotl are amphibians, they actually develop differently than common amphibians that we know, such as frogs and toads. Instead, they develop in the same way as newts and other salamanders. What this means is that instead of developing their back legs first, it is their front legs that develop first.

After a few more weeks, two to three, the hind legs of the axolotl will begin to develop and when they are fully grown, the axolotl will be a juvenile.

During the juvenile stage, the axolotl will look exactly like it will as an adult. The only difference is size. The juvenile will usually be about 50mm in size when it finally develops its hind legs.

After that stage, the axolotl will stay in the juvenile stage for 7 months to 2 years when it becomes sexually mature. Males tend to become sexually mature at an earlier age than females.

By the time the axolotl is an adult, it should be between 8 to 12 inches in length. Some axolotls have been known to grow larger, some as large as 17 inches in length, but this is a rare occurrence.

One thing that is interesting to note is that size can be reflective of the habitat that they grew in. Optimal water temperatures, ideal water quality and an abundance of food will produce larger axolotl. In addition, warmer temperatures tend to create larger axolotl and they will often mature faster in these conditions as well.

## 4. Sexing an Axolotl

Sexing an axolotl can be a difficult task when the axolotl are young. During that time, there are few indicators that show whether the axolotl is male or female. Even as adults, this can be difficult as well.

When you are sexing younger axolotl, you want to look at the vent of the axolotl. This is an area that is found directly behind the back legs close to where the tail and body connect. It is found on the underside of the axolotl.

The vent on the male and female are slightly different and it can be difficult for someone new to axolotls to distinguish between the two. The female axolotl should have a small bump where the vent is. This is a small gland in the cloacal region that creates this.

The male axolotl will have a bump in the cloacal region as well but it will be much larger in the male than in the female.

Once the axolotl matures fully, it is easier to distinguish between male and female. Males have a longer body and tail than females in general. In addition, the male body tends to be straight and narrow.

Females, on the other hand, have a rounded body when they are sexually mature. This is caused by the eggs that are being produced in the female.

They are the only differences that you will see with your axolotl. Again, it can be difficult for a new axolotl owner to distinguish between male or female, however, as you become more familiar with the species, you should be able to determine gender quite easily.

# *Chapter 4. The Axolotl Personality*

Diverse, interesting and unique are three words that describe the personality of the axolotl. This is an animal that is full of personality and it is different for each one.

In fact, the axolotl has a personality that is as varied as people and you never know what type of personality you will get when you bring them home. What you do know is that your interactions with the axolotl will help shape your axolotl's personality.

For instance, if you bring the axolotl home and leave it to itself, never interacting with it and basically ignoring it – you will end up with an axolotl with a wild personality that is very skittish. However, if you play with the axolotl, hand feed him and interact on a daily basis with your pet, you will find that the axolotl is quite playful and engaging.

While your interactions can help shape the personality and temperament of your axolotl, there are some factors that will remain, as these are unique creatures with individual personalities.

In general, axolotl are very curious animals. They love to explore and they will often spend hours exploring their tank. Putting in items that they can play with or interact with is actually very good for your axolotl. They love figuring things out and can spend hours of their day exploring the new item that you put in the tank.

Some axolotl are very outgoing animals. They love attention and they quickly learn that you are going to provide them with both stimulation and food. Many axolotl owners have commented on the fact that their axolotl will tap on the glass of the aquarium in an effort to get the attention of their owners.

In addition, when the owner comes to the aquarium, they will float up to the top of the water and wait to be fed. Some will even pose for photos when they see a camera in hand and this makes them a very interesting pet to have.

Axolotl are known for being very intelligent animals. They will quickly learn basic tricks that are associated with the feeding wand. People have had great success in having the axolotl float to the top or swim a little pattern when the wand is seen near the water. It is important to note that they do not react to verbal commands and the tricks are very basic, similar to ones that you would teach a fish.

But that being said, the level of interaction that you can get with your axolotl is very enjoyable. They will often be eager to see their owner and will be excited when the feeding stick is at hand.

Axolotl can be very clown like and silly in the tank and it can be enjoyable to watch them interact with each other and with the items in the tank.

They are a predatory animal so they will hunt fish that are placed in the tank. In addition, they have been known to eat younger axolotl so it is important to only place individuals that are close to the same size.

While they are carnivores, they are not usually aggressive and owners can often place their fingers in the tank with them. A word of warning, they will, occasional, attach to a finger but they do not have the jaw strength to do any damage with their teeth. All you need to do is wait for the axolotl to spit out your finger, which can be quite comical to watch.

Generally, axolotl can live in tanks with one or two other axolotl but they are not meant for large colonies. Some axolotl can be aggressive to each other, but usually, they do well with axolotl companions. They will often pile onto one another and interact throughout the day. Occasionally, however, they will nip each other and can damage gills, toes and tails.

While your interaction with an axolotl can affect how the axolotl is, there are some axolotl that are naturally skittish. This means that the axolotl will hide when you come near the tank.

In addition, they will often spend much of their time inside their hideouts, which are items where the axolotl can hide from anything it sees as a predatory. Although skittish axolotl are not as enjoyable as their more personable counterparts, as they are usually hidden, they can still be an enjoyable pet and some of the enjoyment is in helping them overcome the skittishness, at least around you.

As you can see, axolotl are very diverse when it comes to personalities. You will get axolotl that are playful, others that are aggressive and some that are shy. They will be outgoing, quiet or silly and this is what makes them such a unique and interesting pet.

# Chapter 5. Preparing for your Axolotl

So you are at that stage of pet ownership and you are ready to start preparing for your axolotl. What an exciting time for you!

Since axolotls are aquatic animals, they will require an aquarium to be happy and healthy. It can be very easy to set up the aquarium but in this chapter, I will go over everything you need to know to make the tank perfect for your axolotl. In addition, I will discuss the requirements for temperature and water quality so your axolotl has the perfect home.

## 1. Your Aquarium

The first thing that I would like to touch on with preparing for your axolotl is how to set up your tank. This is usually the most important thing that you should have set up before you bring your axolotl home. Later on in this chapter I will go over the two different types of tanks that you can use with an axolotl but for now, I want to go over the basic things you will need to know regardless of the type of tank you are setting up.

First, you should consider the size of your aquarium. On average, the axolotl can grow from 8 to 12 inches in length. This means that they need a fair amount of room and the larger your aquarium, the more activity you will see from our axolotl.

A rule of thumb that I have with aquarium size is that if your axolotl cannot turn around in the aquarium, then it is too small. On average, you want 10 gallons of tank space for every adult axolotl that you have.

I recommend keeping no more than two axolotls in one tank; however, some enthusiasts have done well with three adult axolotls in the tank. Again, add 10 gallons in size for every adult that will be in the tank. Remember that this is the bare minimum of space needed so if you have a larger tank, your axolotl will be much happier than in a smaller tank.

In addition to size, you need to consider what type of material your tank will be made of. In today's market, there are a lot of different materials from plastics to glass and it really is up to you what you want to have your tank made of.

For axolotls, I do not recommend any plastic fish tanks, as the majority of plastic tanks are small tanks designed for one or two small fish such as goldfish or a beta.

So with that in mind, you are really only left with two different types of tanks – glass and Plexiglas.

### Glass Aquariums:

Glass is often the go to choice for anyone who is interested in starting an aquarium. They can be found in a number of different sizes and they are usually high quality. The glass is tailored to withstand the weight of water in a filled tank.

In addition, glass usually has a clearer view into the aquarium and is less prone to scratches when you are cleaning it. On the down side, glass is usually very heavy and very expensive. In addition, you can only purchase a square or bowed glass tank and this keeps you from having an interesting tank shape.

Lastly, glass can be broken very easily and there is always the risk of that occurring.

### Plexiglas Aquariums:

33

Plexiglas aquariums have come a long way and have nearly caught up to glass when it comes to quality. While they tend to be a bit cloudy when you are trying to view the axolotl, if you purchase a high quality Plexiglas, you won't be able to notice it.

There are actually a number of benefits when it comes to Plexiglas. First, it can be shaped into any design that you want, which can make an interesting art piece for your tank. In addition, it is more durable and sturdy than glass and it is not as heavy or expensive.

On the down side, Plexiglas is not as clear as glass. In addition, it is more difficult to clean. Lastly, Plexiglas tends to scratch much easier than a glass aquarium and you will quickly notice the wear and tear on the piece, especially if your axolotl likes to tap on the sides of the aquarium.

When it comes to tanks, I recommend glass. They are worth the added expense because glass gives you the best view of your pet.

### a) Setting up any Aquarium

When it comes to setting up your aquarium, it doesn't have to be too difficult. In fact, it can be very easy but regardless of what you are putting it in, whether it is fish or axolotl, I recommend following these steps.

1. Always clean the tank thoroughly before you add anything into it. If it is an old tank, it should be disinfected to ensure that there is no disease present in the tank. There are several axolotl safe disinfectants that you can purchase at many aquarium stores. If it is new, it should still receive a thorough cleaning.

When you are cleaning a tank, make sure that you do not use harsh chemicals, as the residue can stay in the tank and poison your axolotl.

2. Always do a check for leaks. This should be done regardless of the age or the number of uses. Occasionally, a seal may be broken on a brand new tank and it doesn't become apparent until you have it filled.

Fill the tank with water and allow it to sit for a few days to make sure that there are no leaks. Don't bother doing anything else with the tank until you know if there is a leak or not.

3. Clean everything that is going into the tank. Whether it is a decoration, a filter or a plastic plant, you should clean the items. Remember, if they are old pieces of equipment, there could be disease on them so make sure you disinfect them. If they are new, you should still wash them to ensure there are no residues on the items.

Cleaning is very important when you are setting up any new tank, as this will help ensure that nothing is getting into your tank that you don't want.

## 2. Setting up a Basic Aquarium

One of the nicest features with axolotl is that they can thrive in an environment with a little or a lot. Really, they can do well in a tank with very little in the way of equipment but also in quite a large tank with lots of features to it. The following described tank is an ideal set up for a beginner who is just getting interested in the axolotl and wants to start out small.

### a) Equipment

With the basic tank, you won't need a lot of extra equipment. In general, the axolotl can live with very little in its tank and this means that you can save on your first tank. This tank is usually a small 10 gallon tank, although you can do it in a larger tank if you would like.

Although you do not have to purchase a lot of extra equipment, I strongly recommend that you take the time to really look at the equipment and purchase the high quality ones. Remember, you get what you pay for and the quality of the equipment can affect the quality of life for your axolotl.

Equipment and supplies that are an absolute must have for your basic set up are:

- *Filter:* Filters are not a must have equipment as axolotls can thrive in aquariums that have no filtration. However, if there is no filter, then you will need to clean the water frequently to ensure that the axolotl has excellent water quality.

There are many different filters out on the market; however, I recommend that you use an Aquaclear or a Marineland filter. They are usually very high quality and they don't break down as quickly as other filters.

With the basic set up, choose a larger filter, as we will not be using a substrate in this set up. As a result, you want a larger filter so the healthy bacteria have a place to grow.

*- Heater:* Heaters are optional as well, as you do not have to have the water higher than 20°C and many times, the natural temperature of the room can maintain the proper temperature in your water.

The only time I recommend a heater is if you tend to have a cooler room or you want to keep the temperature at a steady level instead of allowing it to fluctuate.

*- Thermometer:* Even if you don't have a heater, make sure that you have a thermometer in the tank so you can keep track of the water temperature. Make sure that you check it frequently and make sure that the temperature stays in the ideal range. If there is a spike or drop in temperature, it could lead to a number of problems for the axolotl.

*- Lid:* There are different types of lids and aquarium hoods that you can purchase for your tank but it is important to have one.

Lids will keep contaminants out of your tank. Air fresheners, dust, and other outside contaminants can land in the water. Even minute traces of some contaminants can destroy the ecosystem in your tank and make your axolotl sick.

In addition to protection, lids offer lighting in the tank. One thing to note is that axolotl do not need light, but to properly see the animal and enjoy your aquarium, you want to have a standard aquarium light in the tank. Try to choose a light that does not emit a lot of heat.

- *Substrate:* With the basic tank, you are not going to want to use any type of substrate on the bottom of the tank. This is a very basic tank and the cleaner it is, the better.

- *Aquarium Gloves:* Finally, make sure that you purchase a good pair of aquarium gloves. This will enable you to place your hands into the aquarium without the worry of contamination from your skin.

## b) Decorations

Although decorations can be viewed as equipment for your aquarium, I feel it is important to look at it separately to ensure that you have the right set up for your axolotl. You can have a number of different decorations in the basic tank but the main focus is to keep it just that – basic.

- *Plants:* With the basic tank, the only decoration that I recommend having is one or two artificial plants. Do not use live plants in a small aquarium, as it can lead to a high level of ammonia, which will make your axolotl sick.

Make sure that the plants you use for your axolotl tank can be suctioned to the bottom of the aquarium. In addition, be prepared to reaffix them. Axolotls are notorious for knocking the plants loose when they are exploring the tank.

- *Natural Terrain:* You can have natural terrain in a basic tank but keep it to the minimum. There are a number of things that you can use, including logs and rocks. Make sure that anything you put in the tank does not have small holes where the axolotl can get stuck under. If you do, this can lead to a lot of serious problems.

With the basic tank set up, I recommend that you use a large stone under the filter to help disperse the current. Axolotls do not do well with strong currents, so you want to keep the filter turned down low.

### c) Hides

Hides are another decoration for your axolotl but it is important to look at them separately. A hide is a must have piece of equipment, whether it is a basic aquarium or a more advanced aquarium.

A hide is a tube, box, or other item that the axolotl can go into to hide. If there is no hide in the aquarium, the axolotl will become stressed by the lack of places to hide when it sees a threat.

Make sure when you use a hide that there are no sharp edges on it where the axolotl could injure itself.

### d) Getting your Tank Ready

Now that you know the various items that you have to have for your aquarium, it is time to start getting it ready. As I have already mentioned, it is very important to wash everything that you are placing in your aquarium. This will help prevent contamination from outside contaminants.

Once you have everything washed, it is time to start setting up your tank. This is not something that I can really guide you through. Read the instructions on any equipment that you have and install it as directed.

Next, do a dry run of how you would like your tank set up. I place the items where I want them. Since there is no substrate that needs to be put in, you don't have to worry about it at all. One thing to mention is that some things need substrate to stay put in the aquarium. If you have an item that may need substrate, choose a different decoration for your tank.

If you are putting in plants, it is best to wait until you have the water in the tank, as some plants need the water to keep from flattening; this is often the case with live plants but you can also see it with plastic or silk plants.

Once you have everything set up, you can begin pouring water in.

When you have the tank filled, you can begin to run your filter and also run your heater, if you have one. You want the water to sit for 1 to 2 days before you add any animal to the tank. This will ensure that the chlorine is out of the water without having to use a dechlorinating chemical.

After the 1 or 2 days, check the temperature on the tank until you get it to the right temperature. When it is at the right temperature, you can begin to cycle your tank, which is how you get the pH levels to the right stage.

Really, when it comes to setting up your tank, all you need to do is put in the equipment, add the water and then do a cycling. Cycling does take time and I will go over the steps you need to take later on in this chapter when I talk about the water quality.

## 3. Setting up an Advanced Aquarium

In the last section, I discussed setting up a basic aquarium for your axolotl and now I am going to talk about setting up an advanced aquarium for your axolotl. When it comes to the advanced set up, you will be using a larger aquarium; at least 50 gallons and you will be using more decorations. In addition, an advanced aquarium uses substrate, which I will discuss later in this chapter.

### a) Equipment

The difference, when it comes to equipment, between the basic tank and the advanced tank, is not a big difference. Really, you will use the same items but you will make sure that they are designed for your tank size.

Like the basic tank, I strongly recommend that you purchase high quality equipment and to have extra on hand in the event that something breaks.

Equipment and supplies that are an absolute must have for your advanced set up are:

- *Filter:* Filters are not a must have equipment as axolotls can thrive in aquariums that have no filtration. However, if there is no filter, then you will need to clean the water frequently to ensure that the axolotl has excellent water quality.

There are many different filters out on the market; however, I recommend that you use an Aquaclear or a Marineland filter. They are usually very high quality and they don't break down as quickly as other filters.

Choose a filter that is designed for your aquarium size and do not go with a larger one. The larger the filter, the heavier the water flow and this can make your axolotl sick.

One thing that I recommend with a filter for an advanced aquarium is to use a spray bar. This is a tube attachment for the aquarium that allows the water to be sprayed across the surface of the tank instead of a heavy stream from the filter.

There are many benefits of a spray bar, including better oxygen dispersal throughout the tank, but the main one is that it will reduce the flow of water for your axolotl.

*- Heater:* Heaters are optional as well, as you do not have to have the water higher than 20°C and many times, the natural temperature of the room can maintain the proper temperature in your water.

The only time I recommend a heater is if you tend to have a cooler room or you want to keep the temperature at a steady level instead of allowing it to fluctuate.

*- Thermometer:* Even if you don't have a heater, make sure that you have a thermometer in the tank so you can keep track of the water temperature. Make sure that you check it frequently and make sure that the temperature stays in the ideal range. If there is a spike or drop in temperature, it could lead to a number of problems for the axolotl.

*- Lid:* There are different types of lids and aquarium hoods that you can purchase for your tank but it is important to have one.

Lids will keep contaminants out of your tank. Air fresheners, dust, and other outside contaminants can land in the water. Even minute traces of some contaminants can destroy the ecosystem in your tank and make your axolotl sick.

In addition to protection, lids offer lighting in the tank. One thing to note is that axolotl do not need light, but to properly see the animal and enjoy your aquarium, you want to have a standard aquarium light in the tank. Try to choose a light that does not emit a lot of heat.

- *Substrate:* Substrate is a difficult choice when it comes to axolotls because they can often swallow it. This can lead to blockages in the digestive system, which is always fatal for the axolotl.

For this reason, there are only a few substrates that I recommend. One is a fine sand substrate. The substrate does not cause blockages in the axolotl if it is swallowed and it can be found in a variety of colours that make it pleasing to the eye.

Another substrate to use is an aquarium sealant, which will be glued to the bottom of the tank. I do not strongly recommend this, as it makes it very difficult to clean the tank.

Never use gravel with an axolotl, as it is gravel that is linked to blockages in the digestive system.

- *Tank Vacuum:* There are many different types of tank vacuums that you can use and it is really something that is a preference. I prefer to use a tank python but you can purchase higher quality tank vacuums. You only need a tank vacuum if you are using substrate.

- *Aquarium Gloves:* Finally, make sure that you purchase a good pair of aquarium gloves. This will enable you to place your hands into the aquarium without the worry of contamination from your skin.

### b) Decorations

Anything can go when it comes to decorations for your advanced aquarium and since you have more room, you can really play around with the placement of the decorations. Some decorations that you can and should have in your axolotl tank are:

*- Plants:* Plants are a must have for your advanced aquarium and you can choose to use either fake or real plants or a combination of both. I have a preference for fake plants as they are easier to manage, however, the size of this tank will allow you to have live plants.

When it comes to plants, there are pros and cons for both and today, fake plants can look just as nice as a real plant.

If you are going with fake, I strongly recommend that you choose silk plants instead of plastic. The reason for this is because they have a more lifelike appearance to them. Another reason is that they tend to be easier to weight down, which will prevent them from floating to the surface.

If you are going with live plants, I recommend that you choose plants that have a thick root system and a broad leaf. This will help prevent the axolotl from uprooting your plants.

*- Regular Tank Decorations:* Tank decorations are usually very common in all aquariums, regardless of whether you have an amphibian or a fish in it. The axolotl aquarium is really no

different and you can place anything that you want in the tank. Make sure that any decorations in the tank are free of sharp edges as axolotl will rub against these things and cut their skin.

In addition, make

sure that there are no small holes where the axolotl will get stuck. You do want to have caves in the tank but you want to make sure that the axolotl can swim out of those caves easily.

*- Natural Terrain:* The last area that you should look into with your decorations is in natural terrain. Logs, rocks, and large shells can be a nice decoration in the tank. In addition, axolotl usually enjoy exploring these natural elements in the tank and it will help with boredom.

Be inventive with what you place in your tank but make sure that it is safe for axolotl. You can also switch it around when you do your weekly cleaning, as axolotl love to explore and will thrive with new settings in the tank.

Lastly, make sure that you clean anything before you put it in your tank.

## c) Hides

Like the basic tank, you will want to make sure that you have hides in your tank. While hides are another decoration for your axolotl, it is important to look at them separately. A hide is a must have piece of equipment, whether it is a basic aquarium or a more advanced aquarium.

A hide is a tube, box, or other item that the axolotl can go into. If there is no hide in the aquarium, the axolotl will become stressed by the lack of places to hide when it sees a threat.

Make sure that when you use a hide that there are no sharp edges on it where the axolotl could injure itself.

With the advanced aquarium, I recommend having two or three different hides available for your axolotl. Spread them out in the tank so that regardless of where he is, he will have somewhere to hide if he feels the need.

### d) Getting your Tank Ready

Now that you know the various items that you have to have for your aquarium, it is time to start getting it ready. As I have already mentioned, it is very important to wash everything that you are placing in your aquarium. This will help prevent contamination from outside contaminants.

Once you have everything washed, it is time to start setting up your tank. This is not something that I can really guide you through. Read the instructions on any equipment that you have and install it as directed.

Next, do a dry run of how you would like your tank set up. I place the items where I want them. Place in the substrate and cover anything that needs to be covered.

If you are putting in plants, it is best to wait until you have the water in the tank as some plants need the water to keep from flattening; this is often the case with live plants but you can also see it with plastic or silk plants.

Once you have everything set up, you can begin pouring water in. The best way is to feed it in with a hose from your tap. If you run the water down the sides of the tank, you will have fewer problems with the sand dispersing through the water and making it cloudy.

When you have the tank filled, you can begin to run your filter and also run your heater, if you have one. You want the water to sit for 1 to 2 days before you add any animal to the tank. This will ensure that the chlorine is out of the water without having to use a dechlorinating chemical.

After the 1 or 2 days, check the temperature in the tank until you get it to the right temperature. When it is at the right temperature, you can begin to cycle your tank, which is how you get the pH levels to the right stage.

## *4. Temperature*

Regardless of whether you are putting together a basic tank or an advanced tank, temperature is a very important factor in your axolotls housing. Although the axolotl is from a warmer climate, it actually does well in cooler water. In fact, many hobbyists have found that axolotl recover from illnesses much better when they are kept in a cooler aquarium.

With temperature, the ideal range for an axolotl is between 16 to 18°C or 60 to 64°F. They can do very well in temperatures close to 10°C or 50°F; however, you will notice changes in the axolotl including:

- Decreased appetite
- Sluggish movement and behavior
- Slower metabolism

While this is not a large problem, it can impede your ability to determine if the axolotl is sick, as the first symptom is often a lack of appetite.

On the opposite end of the temperature index, your axolotl should never be in temperatures above 22°C or 72°F. Anything over that temperature and the axolotl will begin to suffer from heat stroke. This means that the axolotl will have the following symptoms:

- Increased metabolism
- Increase in appetite that becomes a refusal of food after stress kicks in.
- Pale patches on the skin

When it comes to temperatures, it is imperative that you maintain the water temperature as best as you can. If you live in warm climates, it is important to keep the axolotl in a cool room. In addition, placing it closer to the floor will help reduce the heat of the water.

Make sure you keep a thermometer in the tank to help check the water temperature on a daily basis. The tank should not fluctuate temperatures as this can put unnecessary stress on your axolotl. Stress can lead to health problems and make the axolotl more susceptible to disease.

It is easier, and much safer, to keep the tank in a cool room, such as in a basement room, and use a heater to bring the temperature up to a steady level. However, if you do not have that option or you live in a climate where it is always warm, you can try to keep the tank cooler by using chillers.

These are very similar to a heater, except it is used to create a cooler water temperature. These are often used in conjunction with a heater so you can create the best ambient temperature possible.

Chillers are used when you live in a hot climate and your tank will be exposed to high temperatures on a daily basis. For climates where high temperatures are not as frequent and don't last as long, you can use frozen water bottles.

To do this, you really want to monitor your water temperatures. A sudden shift can be as detrimental to your axolotl's health as too much heat. Instead of using a large bottle, use several small ones. Place them in the freezer and then, when your temperature rises too much, use them. To use the water bottles follow the steps below.

1. Place a water bottle into the water; try to keep it to the side of the tank.

2. Monitor the temperature of the water as the bottle is floating in the tank.

3. Allow the bottle to dethaw, meaning leaving the ice to melt. I recommend taking it out when it has dethawed half way instead of leaving it in until it is fully dethawed. If you wait until it thaws out completely, you will see too many fluctuations in the water temperature.

4. Check the temperature.

5. If the temperature is still high, replace the half frozen bottle with a fresh frozen bottle.

6. Repeat until the water temperature is at the desired level. Repeat the process as needed but don't allow the water to climb too much before you try to cool it again.

## 5. Water Quality

Water quality is one of the most important factors in maintaining the health of your axolotl. Poor water quality can affect growth as well as health; however, it can be very easy to properly maintain the water quality of your tank. Later in this chapter, I will discuss keeping the levels at the right level through cleaning, but for now, let's go over everything you need to know about water quality.

### a) Water Flow

One of the biggest mistakes that new axolotl owners make is with water flow. Many feel that there should be good water flow from the filter, however, axolotl do not do well with a strong current or water flow.

In fact, axolotl can often become stressed by a strong water flow and this stress will lead to a decrease in health and an increase in susceptibility to illnesses.

To decrease the flow of water, I recommend the following tips.

### Tip Number One: Use a Spray Bar

A spray bar is a tube attachment for the filter that allows the water to be sprayed across the surface of the tank instead of a heavy stream from the filter. This will help reduce the water flow in your tank very quickly.

### Tip Number Two: Choose a filter that has a flow dial

Another option is to choose a filter where you can reduce or increase the flow of water running through it. This can make it much better for your axolotl and it will still do the work of keeping your aquarium clean.

### Tip Number Three: Change the direction of the water flow

Angling the water filter so the direction of the water flow is different can change the actual water flow in the aquarium. I recommend either angling it so the water flow is directed against the side of the tank or so that it is directed towards the surface of the water. Both angles will reduce the water flow.

### Tip Number Four: Use a smaller filter

Another way to decrease water flow is to use a smaller filter for your aquarium. Usually I recommend going down one tank size. The smaller filter will reduce the amount of water going through the filter and the flow will be smaller when it is done.

### *Tip Number Five: Use filter wool to obstruct part of the flow*

Finally, you can use filter wool to obstruct the filters output. This means that the water flow is not as hard. One of the biggest problems with this tip is that it will cause your filter to wear out much faster than it would under normal use.

The key with all of these tips is to find a way to reduce the flow of water so the axolotl has a clean tank but no strong current to fight.

### *b) Acidity*

Acidity, which is also referred to as pH, is actually the amount of hydrogen ions in the water. The term, pH, refers to the "power of hydronium" and is a look at the acidity and also at the alkalinity in the water. When we look at pH, we are actually looking at a

number; the higher the number, the more acidity in the water.

PH is considered to be neutral when it is at 7. This means that there is neither too much acidity or too little. An axolotl thrives in water that has a pH level of between 6.5 and 8.0. The ideal is a pH level of 7.4 to 7.6.

To adjust the pH in your aquarium, use a pH kit that is sold at aquarium stores. These are safe to use with axolotls and will make it much easier to maintain the proper pH levels for your pet.

### c) Chlorine

I have already mentioned this several times but chlorine is not good for your axolotl. In fact, it can be severely harmful and can lead to a lot of problems for your animal. In the section on health, I have gone over one of the side effects of having chlorine in the aquarium – chlorine poisoning.

In general, you should not have to worry about chlorine if you use a dechlorinator or if you allow the water to stand for at least 24 hours. After a few days of standing, the chlorine in tap water should be eliminated.

One thing that I recommend for axolotl owners is to use Aquarium Pharmaceuticals' Stress Coat on a regular basis whenever you change the water. This will help keep a good mucus on the skin and this will prevent any adverse reactions if there are still minute levels of chlorine in the water when you make the change.

### d) Chemicals

When it comes to chemicals in an aquarium, there is actually a large list of them that you can use. However, I am not going to give you that list because they do nothing for your axolotl in the long run. In fact, they can be quite dangerous to them and I only recommend using amphibian safe chemicals in your tank, if you use them at all.

Instead of being helpful, chemicals often cause unnecessary expenses and most of the time, they can be harmful to your axolotl if you are not using them properly.

The only thing that I recommend you purchase for your aquarium water at this point is water testing strips or a water testing kit. Test strips will help you test the pH levels in your water to ensure that is ideal for your axolotl.

You can purchase chemicals to raise and lower the levels as needed; however, I strongly recommend that you cycle your tank instead of adding the chemicals. It does take longer but it will ensure that your tank has ideal conditions without a lot of added cost. I will discuss cycling your tank in the final section of this chapter.

## 6. Cycling the Tank

As I have mentioned, there is a way to get your water quality to the right levels without having to use chemicals in your aquarium. This process does take a bit longer than chemicals and you will not be able to add an axolotl to your tank until after 30 days.

To properly cycle your tank, there are a few steps that you should take.

### Step One: Fill the Tank

As I have already mentioned, fill the tank with water. You can use filtered water but I find it is less expensive and more practical to use tap water. Once it is full, allow it to sit for a few days until the chlorine has been removed. This is very important before you move to the next stage of cycling.

### Step Two: Add in a Few Fish

The next step that you should take is to add a few fish to your tank. It is important that you choose some cheaper fish from the pet store. Cloud minnows are usually a good choice as they can survive cooler temperatures and they are less likely to bother your axolotl if they happen to still be alive when you add an axolotl.

I don't recommend using extremely cheap fish, as you want to try to avoid introducing any parasites to your tank. Cheap fish are housed in poor conditions so you will find that they have more health problems that can affect your tank.

Fish that you can use are large tetras, cloud minnows or small barbs. You want to make sure that they are known as a hardy fish, as the conditions in your tank are going to get very poor as you are going through the cycling process.

Add the fish according to the species and the gallons. You want to have a good number of fish but not too many that the tank is overpopulated.

### Step Three: Test the Water Daily

Make sure you test the water levels on a daily basis. This will help you with moving forward in the cycling process. You can also watch your fish, as they will become stressed the worse the water gets. The fish in the tank will be releasing ammonia and that is what you want.

### Step Four: Feed the Fish

Feed the fish according to the species. You want them to be healthy but you also want to leave them a little hungry, as hungry fish tend to expend more ammonia since their stomachs are smaller. You want to make sure that you do not overfeed the fish and also make sure that there is no excess food floating in the tank. Any food the fish don't eat will only pollute your tank, which will mean you have to start from the beginning.

### Step Five: Change the Water Slightly

During the first few days, your fish may be surviving fine. By day three, the bacteria in the tank will be established but it will be at very low levels. What this means is that the ammonia will be really high but the bacteria is starting to do its job. As the bacteria eats the ammonia, it begins to change it into nitrates, which will help balance your water levels.

By day 5, you may see some of the less hardy fish die. When you see this, you want to change some of the water to help alleviate the levels of ammonia. To do this, remove only 20% of the water from the tank. You can remove less but do not remove more.

Replace the water that you took with fresh water. Make sure you use water that is free of chlorine, as this will affect your water quality and you will end up having to start from scratch.

You can add clean water to the tank whenever you feel that the fish are getting stressed from the water conditions. Do not do it every day but once a week should be fine. In addition, make sure that you only remove 20% of the water any time you change it.

Usually, you will find that the water levels are dangerous to your hardy fish on Day 5 and Day 14 but it will be different depending on the number of fish that you have in the tank and the size of your tank.

### Step Six: Continue to Monitor Levels

The final step is to continue monitoring the levels in your tank. The goal is to create a good level of bacteria in your filtering system. You don't have to add a lot of different things into the tank, as the fish are creating the proper levels on their own.

When you look at the timeline of those 30 days, you should see something very similar to this.

*- Prior to cycling:* Water is aged enough for the fish to be placed in. In areas where you have high chlorine levels in your tap water, you may need to leave it for up to 7 days.

*- Day 1:* Hardy fish are added to the tank.

*- Day 3:* Healthy bacteria begin to be established in your aquarium at low levels.

*- Day 5:* High level of ammonia, some of your hardy fish may die. You can change some of the water.

*- Day 8:* First level of bacteria is established, ammonia begins to lower and nitrites rise. Fish are happier and more active.

*- Day 14:* Nitrite levels are high. Fish appear stressed again. Second stage bacteria occur, but are still in low supply so it does not affect the nitrite levels. Water can be changed, again, make sure it is only 20%.

*- Day 29:* Second stage bacteria are established and are turning the nitrites into nitrates. The water becomes more habitable for more delicate fish.

After day 29, you should have two types of bacteria in the tank. One type will eat the ammonia produced by fish and turn it into nitrites. The second type will turn the nitrites into nitrates.

Monitor your tank until you get the desirable readings for pH and then add your fish when it has levelled out.

As I said, it is a long process but after you are finished, you will have a perfectly balanced tank that is natural and free of a lot of harsh chemicals.

Once your tank is cycled, your tank set up is complete and you are ready to add your axolotl.

# *Chapter 6. The Axolotl Community*

You have the tank and the axolotl but you are probably wondering what the next step is. Many people are often eager to create a community for their axolotl when they finally have their tank established.

Before you move any new guests into your axolotl aquarium, there is one important piece of advice that I want to give you. That is "Do Not Mix your Species".

This is imperative and is something that I urge people to consider seriously. Axolotl are susceptible to a wide variety of parasites and keeping them in a tank with other species, specifically with fish, can create a hostile environment for your axolotl.

For that reason, there really isn't a lot that we need to go over in regards to the axolotl community; however, there are a few things that I do want to touch on.

### *Fact Number One: Axolotl are Predators*

The first fact that we need to look at with the axolotl community is that axolotl are predators. What this means is that anything you put in the tank can and will be considered as food. They will hunt any fish that you put in.

In addition, they may become cannibals to their own kind, especially if adult axolotl are left in an aquarium with young or smaller axolotl.

### *Fact Number Two: Axolotl can be kept Together*

While they are young, you can keep a large number of axolotl in the same aquarium. They usually do well together and there shouldn't be too many problems. The only thing you should remember is to try to keep the same sized axolotl together to ensure that you do not have incidences of cannibalism occuring.

When the axolotl get larger, it is better to keep two or three together, depending on the size of your aquarium.

### *Fact Number Three: Keep Males and Females Separated*

Females will breed several times a year; however, it is not healthy for them to do so. As a result of this, you should never keep males and females in the same aquarium together. Instead, you should keep males with males and females with females.

The only time that axolotl of the opposite sex are kept together is when they are breeding. For more information on breeding your axolotls, read the chapter on axolotl breeding.

### *Fact Number Four: Do not Mix with other Amphibians*

Just as you would with fish, you should never mix axolotl with other animals or amphibians. Axolotl can be susceptible to disease and parasites in other animals and the best way to avoid cross contamination is to keep them separate.

Another big reason why they shouldn't be housed together is because every species has their own needs when it comes to aquarium set ups.

**Fact Number Five: Axolotl do well Alone**

Finally, axolotl do extremely well when they are left alone and they can be kept in a tank away from other axolotl without any repercussions. While you may want a community tank, don't feel obligated to have one. Instead, enjoy the axolotl that you do have and all of his unique personality.

# 1. Introducing a Second Axolotl

Although I have mentioned that you can enjoy a tank with just one axolotl, you can introduce more than one to a tank. This can be done at the same time or at different times and it is actually quite easy.

One thing that I must stress is that when you are planning to add an additional axolotl to your tank community, you will need to have to places for your axolotl to hide. This means that each axolotl will have a separate hiding spot.

Another thing that you should consider is the size of your tank. Remember, the larger your tank, the more likely your axolotl will adapt to having more than one in the tank.

After that, there really is nothing that you can do but add your axolotl. Before you do, however, make sure that you follow these steps:

- If it is a new axolotl that you have purchased, place it into a quarantine tank for a few weeks until you are sure that there is no parasite or disease. In the chapter on caring for your axolotl, I have gone over how to quarantine your salamander.

- After quarantine, place the new axolotl into the tank and allow the axolotl to get to know eachother.

- Watch the tank. Do not leave the axolotl alone for the first few hours. Instead, watch them to make sure that neither axolotl becomes aggressive. If one does, chase them away from each other if it becomes too violent. It is important to note that aggression between axolotl is very rare and only a few cases have been documented.

After a few hours, or often days, the axolotl will begin to relax around each other. Most often, they become companions and will often lie side by side or on top of one another in the tank, making the community a very positive one.

# Chapter 7. Caring for your Axolotl

Once you have your
aquarium set up and
your axolotl in it, there
really is not a lot that
you need to know
about the everyday
care of the axolotl. In
fact, the axolotl is a
very easy to care for
animal that has few
needs when it comes to
daily care.

A quick checklist of care that you should give your axolotl is as
follows:

*- Feeding:* Feeding should be done once a day for younger
axolotl and two to three times per day for juvenile axolotl. Adult
axolotl can usually be fed every other day, however, I
recommend a once a day schedule.

*- Water Testing:* Water quality is imperative in maintaining the
health of your axolotl and it should be done several times per
week. The key to preventing a lot of diseases is to properly test
the water and catch spikes in levels quickly.

*- Cleaning the Tank:* Later on in this chapter, I will go over
cleaning the tank but it is something that should be done weekly
and then once a month a thorough clean should be done.

And that is about it. If you do hand feeding with your axolotl, you
will interact with him and provide him with stimulation. It is
important that you never handle an axolotl if you can avoid it.

They have extremely sensitive skin and handling can injure your axolotl.

While they can be an amazing pet, these are not pets that you can handle and should be treated in the same way that you would treat a fish.

## *1. Transporting Your Mexican Salamander*

One question that I am often asked is how do you transport your axolotl when you first purchase one. Many people are unsure how to properly transport them and because of this, they end up causing unnecessary stress to the axolotl.

Before you worry too much, however, I want to let you know that transporting an axolotl is actually quite simple. All it requires is a few tools that will make it less stressful for your axolotl.

When it is time to transport your axolotl, make sure you look at your axolotl and assess his health. Read the chapter on the Axolotl health to know the signs of disease.

Once you have determined that he is healthy, you can begin preparing him for your transportation or move.

First, purchase a Styrofoam box. Many pet stores have these and you can often get them for free at the store. If you can't, purchase a Styrofoam cooler. Make sure that it is long enough for your axolotl to be comfortable in it.

Next, fill a bottle of water and place it in the freezer until it is frozen. It is important to note that you will only need to do this if the temperature is over 21°C or 70°F.

When you have everything ready, it is time to get your axolotl ready for transporting. First, get a 2 millilitre flat plastic bag from a fish store. You want to get one that is long, about 15 inches in length and about 8 inches in width.

Carefully remove your axolotl from the aquarium with a net. Place inside the empty bag.

Fill the bag a 1/3 of the way full with water from the aquarium. You want to make sure that you have enough water in the bag so it covers the axolotl when he is lying flat in the bag.

Add air to the bag, usually 2/3rds of the bag will be filled with air. The best way to accomplish this is to take a bike pump and pump up the bag.

Twist the bag closed and fold it over before securing it with a rubber band. Cover the first bag with a second bag, covering in the opposite direction as the first. Twist closed and secure with a rubber band. The reason why you double bag the axolotl is so you have more security. If the first bag bursts, the second bag will keep your axolotl safe.

Once your axolotl is in the bag, add a layer of packing peanuts to the bottom of the Styrofoam box. Place the axolotl in the centre of the box and pour packing peanuts around the axolotl until it is secure. You don't want the axolotl to move around in the box.

Cover the axolotl bag completely with the peanuts and then place the frozen water bottle down the side of the box. Make sure that it does not go directly against the axolotl bag. If it touches directly, it could lead to the axolotl becoming too cold. Only use the frozen water bottle if it is hot outside. It will keep the axolotl cool and will also slow its metabolism, which will alleviate some of the stress.

Close the lid of the Styrofoam box and tape it with packing tape so there is no chance of the box flipping open as you are transporting it.

That is all there is to do to transport your axolotl. It is very simple and while it may seem involved, transporting them in this manner will ensure that they will feel the least amount of stress, even if the trip is several hours.

## *2. Creating Entertainment*

One of the most important parts of caring for your axolotl is to give the axolotl opportunity to really enjoy itself and explore. Although many people are not aware of this when they first start with axolotl, they are actually very inquisitive animals.

What this means for the axolotl owner is that your axolotl can become bored if it is left in a tank with very little to do. That is why it is important to mix things up a bit in the terrain.

Some ways to do that are:

*1. Add new items on a regular basis.* One of the first things you can do is add new things to the aquarium on a regular basis. This could be decorations, plants, or natural terrain. The main point is that the new item gives the axolotl something to explore so be creative with it – just make sure that it is safe and thoroughly cleaned.

*2. Remove items that are ignored.* If you find that your axolotl looks bored with some of the items in the tank, remove them for a little while. You can reintroduce them again later on but you want to keep the axolotl entertained by switching the items that are boring it.

**3. Rearrange the furniture.** Just like people, who need to rearrange their furniture from time to time, an axolotl will need to have a bit of a change up when it comes to their aquarium. I recommend mixing it up once a month when you do a thorough cleaning. While most of the terrain will be the same, your axolotl will enjoy himself swimming around and exploring the new set up.

Remember that keeping your axolotl entertained will help in keeping it happy and healthy.

## 3. Aquarium Care

The final thing that we are going to look at is maintaining the aquarium. This is very important when it comes to axolotl care and is one of the most time consuming aspects of owning an axolotl.

A properly maintained aquarium will ensure that your animal remains healthy. Remember that the health and happiness of an axolotl is tied directly to the quality of the water and the home that he lives in. If you don't maintain a proper home, your axolotl will become sick.

When it comes to aquarium care and maintenance, there are three rules that you should follow. These are:

### 1. Minimize the number of animals in the tank.

This is very important for two reasons. One, axolotl do not do well with other species, especially fish, as they will prey on the fish or the fish will nibble their toes and gills. Two, too many animals will cause a spike in nitrate levels, which will affect the overall water quality and can lead to several illnesses.

### 2. Do scheduled water changes.

Although many people feel that you can simply add the water and leave it, this is not the case. Do a partial water change several times per month. Take out 20% of the water from the tank and discard it. Once you discard it, fill the tank with dechlorinated water. This will help keep ammonia, nitrates and nitrites at respectable levels. In addition, it will help keep your filter working properly.

### 3. Do not overfeed.

Lastly, make sure that you do not overfeed your axolotl. If you do, you will find that it is difficult to keep the aquarium clean and the water quality will be very poor. This will lead to a higher chance of disease in your aquarium and your fish may begin dying because of it.

I find that it is better to hand feed an axolotl since you can keep the decaying food to a minimum when you do. If you simply toss the food into the aquarium, some of it will be missed and this will lead to your tank becoming dirty.

If you are following these three rules with your aquarium, you will find that you will only need to deal with the aquarium care once a week.

Once a week, do a light cleaning. When you do a light cleaning, you should do the following steps:

1. Take an aquarium safe cloth and wipe the front and sides of the glass on the outside.

2. Take a second aquarium safe cloth and wipe the inside of the glass to wipe away any residue that has formed on the glass in the water.

3. At this point, if you have gravel or sand substrate, take your gravel vacuum and vacuum the gravel. You want to remove as

much dirt and debris from the gravel, as this is usually where food is left by the axolotl. The food will decay and lead to higher levels of ammonia in the tank.

4. While you are vacuuming, change about 10 to 20% of the water. This can be done every ten days but I find that it is much easier to do it weekly. Make sure you replace the water with dechlorinated water.

That is really all you need to do on a weekly basis. Every two to eight weeks, you will need to clean and change the filter. In addition, you should remove the carbon in the filter when you are doing the filter cleaning.

Once a month, however, you should do an intense cleaning on your axolotl aquarium. This means that about 50% of the water should be drained from your tank minus the water you are storing your axolotl in.

1. Remove your axolotl from the tank and place it in a clean bucket or aquarium while you are cleaning. Use some of the water from his normal aquarium so he isn't shocked by a sudden water change.

2. Drain out 50% of the water in the aquarium.

3. When it is drained, take the time to wash all of the sides of the aquarium and the bottom with a reptile/amphibian friendly cleaner.

4. Remove all of the substrate and decorations while you are cleaning.

5. Rinse the substrate until all of the debris is off of it. Return the clean substrate to the clean aquarium.

6. Wash all of the decorations with reptile/amphibian friendly cleaners. This is one of the main reasons why I prefer plastic plants as opposed to live, as they are easier to clean.

7. Once everything is clean, reassemble the aquarium until it looks the way you want it.

8. Refill the aquarium with clean, distilled water until it is at the desired height.

9. Return your axolotl to the tank and enjoy until the next time you have to clean the tank.

Although it may seem like a pain, having the proper care for your axolotl, including having a properly cleaned tank, will ensure that your pet stays healthy and happy.

## *Chapter 8. Your Axolotl's Diet*

One thing that I am often asked regarding axolotls is whether they are difficult to feed or not. While you can have some challenges with feeding, generally, they are not that difficult  to feed and there are many different foods that you can offer to them.

It is important to note that this chapter covers the diet of an adult axolotl; it does not cover the diet of a juvenile axolotl or axolotl that are in the larvae stage. In the chapter on breeding, I will go over the foods that you should be feeding your axolotl when it is young.

For now, let's look at the diet of an axolotl after it has reached some size, usually larger than 2 inches. For those of you who are not aware of it, axolotls are carnivores. This means that they solely eat meat and do not eat any vegetation.

While this is excellent when it comes to maintaining your tank plant life, it also means that you have a challenge in providing a well rounded diet for your axolotl.

Before we look at the diet itself, it is important to understand the axolotl's mouth. The axolotl has a cup like mouth that is known as a ambystoma. This mouth is perfect for sucking up food quickly in a vacuum like motion before swallowing. While they do have teeth in their mouth, designed specifically for griping, the axolotl does not have the ability to bite or chew with those teeth. For that reason, it is imperative that you match the food with the size of the axolotl that you own.

Axolotls are predators and this is very apparent when they are young. In fact, young axolotls will not eat anything but live food. Adults, however, will eat both live and dead food and they will also eat pellets that are manufactured specifically for salamanders.

There are a number of pros and cons for feeding live food to your axolotls. One pro is that axolotls do enjoy hunting and are predators. This is a way to provide them with something to do in their tank. Another pro is that the axolotl can get all their nutritional needs from a range of live food, making it easier to maintain their health. Third, live food can be inexpensive compared to pellets. Axolotls will eat wild food such as earthworms so it does offer you a number of different ways to obtain food for your salamander.

The biggest con with live food is that many contain parasites that can be harmful to your axolotl. The best way to prevent this is to avoid wild species and to raise them or farm them on your own.

Feeding of the axolotl will range depending on your individual axolotl and their growth. When they are fully grown, you shouldn't have to feed them more than once every two days. While they are growing, they should be fed daily.

## 1. Types of Food

Now that you know a few of the insights into the axolotl's eating habits, it is time to look at the different foods that your axolotl can eat.

**- *Blackworms:*** These are a small, dark brown worm that are found in aquatic habitats, which is why they are perfect for axolotl. They are filled with lots of nutrients and they can be a staple food for axolotl.

Black worms themselves are very thin and small and they often make a good choice for axolotl that are younger and still growing, as they can be swallowed easily. It is better if you create your own colony of blackworms or purchase them from a pet store, as the wild variety of blackworms can contain parasites that will make your axolotl sick.

**- *Earthworms:*** If you are looking for a super food for your axolotl, then look no further than earthworms. They are filled with a high level of nutrients and are quite large, which fills your axolotl quickly.

Earthworms can be purchased or they can be obtained as easily as picking them out of a garden. One warning with earthworms is that it is important to find them in organic gardens or to create a worm farm and use them from there. Worms that are pulled from regular gardens will have a high level of chemicals in their system and this could poison your axolotl.

**- *Whiteworms:*** While many owners of axolotl love whiteworms, I do not recommend them as a staple food. This is a great food that can be used as a treat or given to juvenile axolotls as a staple food since they are high in fat. They are usually easy to find, but again, try to find a farmed variety to help prevent the spread of any parasites, which are often found in wild species.

**- *Bloodworms:*** These are actually a type of larvae and are not actually a worm, although they look a bit like a worm. They are usually an excellent food for axolotl and they can be purchased both alive and dead. In fact, you can usually purchase frozen bloodworm cubes, which are perfect for younger axolotl.

One thing to remember with bloodworms is that they can be found in the wild, which will reduce the amount of money that you are spending on your feed. However, wild varieties of

bloodworms can carry parasites that will make your axolotl very sick.

Another thing to remember with bloodworms is that they have a bright red coloration, which can cause the water to become dirty when they are eaten.

*- Pellets:* If you want a balanced diet without having to worry about live animals, then you can use pellets. There are salamander pellets on the market, but at this time, I am not overly impressed with them.

Instead, I recommend that you choose a fish pellet that has a high level of protein and is fortified with vitamins. Size is very important when you choose a pellet and you should never choose one that is larger than 5mm in diameter. In addition, if your axolotl is young, never choose a pellet larger than 3mm.

With the pellet, you want one that has about 45% protein. Most pellets will have nutritional values on the package so it isn't too hard to find the ratios. Fat content should never be higher than 20%. Remember, too much fat will cause a dietary imbalance and can affect the health of your axolotl.

## 2. Treats for your Axolotl

As you can tell, there are a number of different foods that you can feed your axolotl as a staple food. They are usually very easy to find and can be quite inexpensive. When it comes to staple foods, it is pretty cut and dry; however, don't feel that you can only feed staple foods.

In fact, you can offer your axolotl a treat every time you feed him and you can make treats a part of hand feeding if you want.

Treats should be given in moderation. Remember that you do not want your axolotl to fill up on the garbage foods since you want him to have a well-rounded meal that has the right amount of vitamins, proteins and fats.

Still, the occasional treat is okay for the average axolotl; however, if he has health problems, make sure that you do not give him too many treats while he is recovering. Treats that you can use with axolotl are:

*- Frozen Brineshrimp:* This could actually be a staple food if it wasn't so hard to maintain and feed an axolotl. Generally, brineshrimp are very difficult to maintain as an individual farm. In addition, transporting them from a brineshrimp breeder can result in the entire shipment dying.

Another problem with brineshrimp is that the frozen variety is very messy when it is eaten. This means that you will have to struggle with the water quality to get it back to normal.

While they do have detractors, this is actually one of the best foods that you can give your axolotl. If you are up to the task of dealing with the cons of this food, then I strongly urge you to consider it as your main staple food. If you aren't, make sure you offer it as a treat a few times per month.

*- Newt and Turtle Food:* Another popular choice for a treat is newt or turtle food. This is sold in a floating food and while it can be a staple food, it often doesn't have the proper nutrients that you should be looking for.

One of the biggest problems with newt and turtle food is that it floats. While this is okay for a range of animals, the axolotl do not like to hunt for their food on the surface of the water. They are less likely to find this food so it is a treat that you will need to offer via hand feeding, which I will go over later on in this chapter.

*- Beef Heart:* The use of beef heart as a treat is one that is widely debated. Some enthusiasts swear by it while others do not. For myself, I find there are pros and cons and it can be a harmless treat for your axolotl.

Generally, beef heart should be a rare treat and it should not be given in large quantities. There really is no nutritional value for your axolotl and it is simply a junk food.

When you do give axolotls beef heart, make sure that you cut it into extremely small pieces; about 5mm or smaller in width and 10mm in length. Hand feed it to the axolotl and give two or three pieces at the most.

*- Feeder Fish:* Many books and websites will recommend feeder fish as an excellent treat; however, I recommend that you avoid them all together. Feeder fish often carry parasites that can be transferred to your axolotl.

*- Grubs:* While they can be difficult to find, grubs are often a favourite treat for axolotl. They are high in fat and offer a good quality protein for your axolotl. I would recommend this as the best treat for your axolotl.

*- Mealworms:* The final treat that you can give your axolotl is a mealworm or two. Again, this treat has little to no nutritional value for the axolotl but they are easy to find. Most pet stores will carry mealworms.

If you are feeding your axolotl mealworms, be aware that they cannot digest the hard exoskeleton of the mealworm. This means that they will expel the exoskeleton into the water and this will lead to you having to remove it from the water and the filter. For this reason alone, I keep mealworms to a minimum.

## 3. Teaching to Hand Feed

Although feeding your axolotl can be as simple as dropping in the food and walking away, many owners like to teach their axolotl to be hand fed.

This can be a wonderful way to interact with your axolotl and it is a fun activity to do. In addition, there is the benefit of knowing exactly how much your axolotl is eating, seeing as you are watching it go into his mouth.

One of the detractors with hand feeding is that you can get bitten. This is scarier than it is harmful, as axolotl do not have the jaw power to properly bite down and cause damage to the human skin. Instead, you might feel a pricking or suction but not actually feel any pain. If you are worried about getting bitten, you can use a feeding rod with your axolotl and train it to take right from the rod.

Although people think it is difficult, training an axolotl can be quite easy. Seeing as they are predators, you simply want to hold the food in your hand and place it in the water.

If the axolotl does not go after the food right away, wiggle your fingers or the food to trigger the "snap". The snap is when the axolotl reacts to movement and does a quick inhale of water, sucking in the food that is in your hand.

Generally, axolotl do not have a shy temperament, especially when it comes to food, and will take food the very first time it is offered. If they don't, continue offering it by hand until it becomes interested in the food. Don't just place the food in the tank and leave it, as the axolotl will become familiar with eating on its own.

Instead, take the food with you and then offer it again in a few hours, again by hand. Repeat until the axolotl takes from your hand. It may take a day or two but the axolotl will eventually take from your hand when he is hungry enough.

Continue feeding your axolotl in this manner until he takes from your hand every time. In addition, as your axolotl becomes accustomed to hand feeding, he will begin to interact with you in the hopes of getting food.

The only other thing that I would recommend is to wash your hands before and after you feed your axolotl to prevent the spread of parasites and diseases.

# *Chapter 9. Your Axolotl's Health*

As any pet owner knows, whether they own a dog, cat or axolotl, health is an important part of pet ownership. The health of the pet will determine what their quality of life will be.

While axolotl are fairly healthy animals, they are also animals that can become ill quite easily. In fact, water quality, food quality and how often they are bred can affect their lifelong health.

In addition, there are diseases that can affect your axolotl so it is important to be aware of health problems. By having the proper knowledge, you can give your axolotl a long and healthy life.

## *1. Keeping Your Axolotl Healthy*

Throughout this entire book, I have gone over everything that you need to keep your axolotl healthy. Really, if you maintain proper care, keep water quality at a healthy level and feed your axolotl a proper diet, you should be able to keep your axolotl healthy.

That being said, there are a few things that you can do to ensure that your axolotl stays healthy and happy throughout its life. One thing that I recommend is that you should always remember five rules. These are:

### *1. Avoid Stress*

Axolotl, like any type of aquatic animal, can suffer from stress. In fact, stressing your animal too much can lead to decreased activity, lethargy and will result in illnesses.

If you are new to aquatic animals, then you are probably not sure what stress entails so it is important to look at it in these terms.

*- Water Levels:* As we all know, poor water quality can be detrimental to the health and happiness of your axolotl. PH levels that fluctuate can create a lot of stress to your pet and any fluctuation in any of the levels, such as low oxygen, can cause stress to your axolotl. This will result in poor health and in severe cases; it can lead to the death of your axolotl. One thing that I always recommend is that you check your water quality on a daily basis.

*- Water Temperature:* This falls in the same category as water levels. Axolotl do live in warmer climates so they are used to warmer water, however, it should not be as warm as a tropical tank. In general, the axolotl should have a temperature of around 18 to 20°C, even though they can be in tanks that are as cold as 10°C. During breeding, you will fluctuate the temperature of the water, however, it should never be higher than 22°C or the axolotl will suffer from heat stress. Try to keep the water temperature steady. If you have constant fluctuations in the water, the axolotl is going to become stressed. Once the axolotl is stressed, its immune system will weaken and it will be more susceptible to illnesses.

*- Tank Set Up:* How you set up your aquarium can also affect your axolotl and cause stress. All axolotl require places to feel sheltered, which is also known as a hide. If there is nowhere for the axolotl to hide, it will begin to feel stressed. For more information on hides and tank set up, read the chapter on preparing for your axolotl.

*- Current:* As you may know, the axolotl does require a current in the tank; however, it must be a light current. Too strong and the axolotl will become stressed and will become sick very quickly.

*- Tank Companions:* Axolotl should never be kept with other species of animals, especially fish. They can do very well with other axolotls but they can become stressed or even pick up parasites from other animals so avoid adding fish or other amphibians, besides one or two other axolotls, to your aquarium.

### *2. Feed a Proper Diet*

We have gone over this in length on our chapter regarding feeding your axolotl. It is very important that you feed your axolotl a proper diet. This means that they should have one or two staple foods that they eat on a regular basis and one or two treats that it gets off and on. Junk foods should be avoided if it is possible.

In addition to a proper diet, it is important that you do not overfeed your axolotl. Axolotl will often gorge themselves on food if it is presented to them. Too much food can lead to health problems, so it is important to avoid this. The general rule of thumb is to only feed your axolotl once a day when he is a young adult, two to three times a day if he is a juvenile and every other day as an adult. With your axolotl, try not to give in to his begging too much...and trust me, they will beg once they realize that you give them food.

### *3. Do not Feed Wild Food*

When it comes to the budget, feeding your axolotl wild food can be very tempting. After all, many of the foods are easy to collect from small ponds or even from a garden during warmer seasons.

However, despite the ease of finding the food, I recommend that you do not feed wild food. The main reason is that they are often filled with parasites that can be transferred to your axolotl, leading to stress and illness. The other reason is that many can be full of chemicals, which again affect your axolotl's health.

If you do choose to use wild food, make sure you find the food in fish free ponds. The only food that I feel you can find in the wild are earthworms. If you do dig for your own earth worms, make sure that you do so from an organic garden.

### 4. Do a Daily Health Test

One of the best ways to keep your axolotl healthy is to really pay attention to it. Check the animal on a daily basis and make sure that there are no signs of disease or illnesses. Often, if you catch an illness early, you can correct the problem without too much damage to your axolotl.

When you are doing a health test, make sure you look the axolotl over completely. Check for damage from the other axolotl in the tank if there are some. For the most part, damage to the skin and limbs are not something to be worried about, as the axolotl does regenerate, however, it is important to watch for signs of infection at the wound site.

In addition, watch for normal gill movement and make sure that your axolotl has normal activity levels.

Another thing to look for is any parasites or external signs of disease. You should also watch your axolotl and make sure that it is moving properly and that there is nothing unusual about the way it moves around the tank.

### 5. Do Not Force the Metamorphosis

One of the interesting facts about axolotl is that they can go through a metamorphosis. This is often done through the use of hormones, however, some will do it spontaneously and no one understands why. When they do go through the metamorphosis, you will be left with a salamander that has different needs than your axolotl.

One thing that I am often asked is how can you force the metamorphosis. While it can be interesting to watch, I strongly recommend that you do not force it. For one, you will no longer have an axolotl in the true sense of the word. For the other, it causes a lot of stress on the axolotl and will weaken it significantly. This weakened state can leave it susceptible to disease and parasites.

If you follow these five rules with your axolotl, you should be able to keep him healthy and happy for a long time.

## 2. Signs of Disease

Before we discuss the diseases and parasites that can attack your axolotl, it is important to understand the signs of disease. There are actually many different signs and they will differ depending on the disease. For more information on signs relating specifically to a disease, read up on the disease itself later in this chapter.

One thing that I recommend every axolotl owner do is a daily health check. This will enable you to look at the overall well being of your pet and will ensure that you catch illnesses early. Remember, the earlier you catch a disease or parasite, the less damage it will do to your axolotl.

When you do a daily health check, look for the following signs:

*1. No appetite:* Loss of appetite is often one of the first signs that you will see when your axolotl is ill. If you find that he has lost his appetite, or doesn't seem to be eating much, then you should monitor him for other symptoms.

*2. Lethargy:* An axolotl that seems to be moving very slowly and does not have the energy levels that it normally has could be suffering from an illness. Watch for other symptoms.

*3. Gill Deterioration:* Many illnesses will attack the gills and you will begin to see the gills deteriorating. This can be a gradual shift in color, a decrease in size or it can be a rapid decay of the gills.

*4. Gill Direction:* This does go hand in hand with the gill deterioration but occasionally, you will see the gills being held in an unusual manner before you see any deterioration. Forward turned gills are a sure sign that the axolotl is stressed, usually due to a heavy current.

*5. Floating near the surface:* Axolotls do not enjoy being near the surface of the water and will only be at the surface occasionally. If you see the animal floating at the surface for a prolonged period, something could be wrong. Sometimes it could be as simple as gas and the axolotl only needs to burp, but other times, it could signal a serious problem.

*6. Loss of mobility:* Another sign is if your axolotl has a sudden loss of mobility. If you see it crashing into decorations or the sides of the tank, check him over for more symptoms. They can be clumsy and when they have a sudden burst of speed, they will collide with objects in the tank; however, if it is a constant loss of mobility and coordination, then it could be an indication that something is wrong.

**7.  *Pale Coloration:*** If the coloration of your axolotl begins to become pale, especially in the gill coloring, then you could be seeing signs of anaemia. Often, anaemia is caused by stress or too strong of a flow of water; however, sometimes anaemia is an indication of another illness. Check the water flow in your tank and other signs of stress before you check for an illness. Often, shifting the flow of water can correct the

anaemia and there is nothing else that needs to be done.

**8. *Jaundice:*** Jaundice is another colour shift that you can see in your axolotl when it is stressed or is becoming ill. Jaundice is the yellowing of the skin pigmentation and it is easier to see on light axolotls. Watch for other symptoms if you see signs of jaundice.

**9. *Open Sores:*** Another indicator that your axolotl is ill is the sudden appearance of open sores on the body. These are not bite wounds but actual sores that burst open. Be sure to check the other symptoms of your axolotl if you see open sores.

**10. *Rapid respiration*:** Finally, if the axolotl looks as though he is gasping for air at any time, he may be suffering from an illness or he may be stressed.

One of the more interesting facts about axolotl health is that illness is usually seen more during the larval stage before they become juveniles. After that stage, the other high risk stage of development is when the axolotl are becoming sexually mature, usually between 7 months to 2 years.

Once they have reached sexual maturity, axolotl are actually quite hardy and if they are cared for properly, they don't usually suffer too many health problems. Females are often at a higher risk of illness than males, specifically because egg production does take a lot of energy. For this reason, you should never breed a female more than twice a year.

In addition to these symptoms, make sure that you know the symptoms of common diseases that can affect your axolotl. By knowing the symptoms, you can treat your axolotl quickly and see him on the road to recovery before the disease does any lasting damage.

## *3. Common Diseases*

As I have mentioned, there are a number of diseases and problems that can affect your axolotl. These diseases can range in severity so it is important to treat them as soon as possible. In this section, I will go over everything you need to know about the diseases affecting your axolotl.

### *a) Metabolic Bone Disease:*

Known as MBD, Metabolic Bone Disease is a term that is used to describe a number of diseases linked together. All of the diseases are caused by an imbalance of nutrients in the axolotl's, body due to an improper diet.

When there is an imbalance, the lack of a specific nutrient disrupts the secretion, absorption and the axolotl's ability to use many different nutrients causing malnutrition. This malnutrition leads to many problems with the axolotl, including bone disease.

### *Symptoms:*

Symptoms of Metabolic Bone Disease can range in severity and symptoms. Some animals seem unaffected by the condition until it has progressed significantly. Others have a high occurrence of symptoms very early on, however, it can be very difficult to distinguish the disease from other problems that the axolotl has.

That being said, there are several symptoms that you can see in the axolotl. These are:

- Curvature of the spine
- Bone Fractures
- Abnormal posture with splayed extremities
- Bloated body
- Deformed jaw: the axolotl cannot close its mouth and looks like it is laughing.
- Low activity levels
- Spasms
- Trembling
- Muscle Cramping
- Intestinal Prolapse

Diagnosing Metabolic Bone Disease can be quite difficult, as it is often overlooked or mistaken for another illness. In addition, many times it can only be successfully diagnosed through the use of an x-ray.

### *Causes:*

As I have already mentioned, one of the main causes for Metabolic Bone Disease is improper nutrition. It is an imbalance of nutrients but it can be caused by specific imbalances. These imbalances are:

*- Calcium Imbalance:* Calcium is an important nutrient for all animals to have, as it used heavily to strengthen the skeleton. A lack of calcium in the diet can cause a severe imbalance in the body and will affect the metabolic processes of the body. It can affect muscle contractions, cell division and will impair vision.

*- Vitamin D Imbalance:* Vitamin D is another important nutrient that helps the axolotl's body absorb and utilize other nutrients. In general, it is very difficult for axolotls to get enough vitamin D as most animals absorb it from UVB. Since axolotls are not exposed to a lot of sunlight, they need it in their diets. In addition, they need the proper levels, as it can accumulate in the body and cause several problems for your amphibian. In deficiency, the body will not be able to absorb calcium.

*- Phosphor Imbalance:* Phosphor works together with calcium to build on the skeletal structure of the axolotl's body. In addition, phosphor aids in regulating the metabolism of the amphibian. When there is an imbalance between calcium and phosphor, it can lead to a breakdown of the skeleton and the condition Metabolic Bone Disease.

*- Vitamin A Imbalance:* Vitamin A is a very important nutrient for axolotl, since it is one of the primary vitamins that help the regeneration process of the axolotl. Without it, regeneration is greatly diminished and with excess, it can begin to affect the liver.

### Treatment:

Treatment will vary depending on the progression of the disease and the nutrient that has the imbalance. Generally, diet is improved to help correct the imbalance. The recommended diet is a varied diet of live food that imitates the axolotl's natural diet as closely as possible.

Another way to help give your axolotl all the nutrients that he needs is to gut load your live food. Gut loading is when you feed the food a vitamin rich feed from the pet store. When the feeder animal is full, you can feed your axolotl and he will get the nutrients in both the feed and the feeder animal.

### b) Wounds

Wounds are a common occurrence with axolotls, especially if they are housed with other axolotls. It is not uncommon for them to be bitten by each other or to damage their body on the decorations in the tank, especially if you have too many decorations in the tank.

### Symptoms:

Although symptoms are very apparent, as it is a wound on the axolotl, make sure you take the time to check the wound. There are some conditions that can lead to open sores so it is important to know the difference between a wound and an open sore.

### Cause:

As I have mentioned, the cause for wounds can be varied and can be the result of decorations in the tank that are too sharp. They can also be caused by other axolotls in the tank. Generally, an axolotl who is housed by himself will have fewer wounds than one that is housed with another animal.

### Treatment:

For the most part, treatment of the wound is very simple, seeing as the axolotl will regenerate it on its own. However, you can help speed up the healing by lowering the water temperature slightly. Although it is unclear why, cooler water tends to

increase regeneration rates, so try to keep the temp at between 10 to 15°C or 50 to 59°F.

Although it is not often needed, you can help prevent infection of the wound by mixing in 1 teaspoon of salt to every 2 litres of water in the tank. Only do this while the wound is healing and stop when it has finished healing.

Finally, it is important to make sure that you keep the tank clean while the wound is healing, as this will help prevent infections and other problems.

### c) Carbon Dioxide Poisoning

Carbon Dioxide poisoning occurs when there is a high level of carbon dioxide in the water. When it is breathed in by the axolotl, it leads to the oxygen carrying pigment in red blood cells to stop transporting oxygen through the animal's body. This leads to several problems including death.

### Symptoms:

Symptoms are often over looked, as they can be quite minor. However, if the symptoms are not seen early enough, it can result in the death of your axolotl. Symptoms include:

- Loss of appetite

- Increased breathing

*Cause:*

Carbon Dioxide poisoning usually occurs as a result of overcrowding in a tank or lack of cleaning the tank. It is often seen more frequently in young axolotls that are housed in large numbers. It may also be seen after transporting an axolotl, since they are housed in a small container for the trip.

*Treatment:*

The best treatment for carbon dioxide poisoning is an influx of oxygen. Place the axolotl in an oxygen rich tank until its health has been restored.

Although placing the axolotl in an oxygen rich tank is beneficial, while the animal is in the tank, it is very important to check the oxygen levels in its primary tank. If they are low, correct it by placing an air pump in the tank.

*d) Nitrate Poisoning*

Nitrate poisoning is very similar to other forms of poisoning that your axolotl can experience such as nitrite and ammonia poisoning.

*Symptoms:*

Symptoms of nitrate poisoning are very serious and if they are not treated as quickly as possible, you could lose your axolotl. Symptoms include:

- Loss of appetite
- Changes in pigment
- Increased Respiration

- Decreased Activity or Lethargy

### *Cause:*

Nitrate poisoning is caused by high levels of nitrates in the tank. This is usually caused by overcrowding, overfeeding and even irregular water changes.

It can also be caused by poor maintenance. Finally, high nitrate levels can occur if you live in an area with high nitrate levels in the drinking water.

### *Treatment:*

Treatment for nitrite poisoning is in correcting the nitrite levels in your tank. This means that you may have to move your axolotl to a new tank that is cycling properly and has low levels of nitrite and ammonia.

While it is in the other tank, remove 20% of the water and replace it with water that is free of chlorine. In addition, clean the tank and find the source for the high nitrate levels so you can remove them.

### *e) Red Leg Bacteria*

This is one of the most common diseases that you will see in an axolotl and it can be quite serious when an axolotl contracts this disease.

### *Symptoms:*

Red Leg bacteria is a very serious condition, where bacteria begins to overwhelm the animal's immune system. This can lead to serious side effects and symptoms and can lead to the animal dying. Symptoms are:

- Loss of appetite
- Red pigment that is under the skin
- Red patches on the body and limbs
- Bloating
- Anorexia
- Lethargy
- Open Sores
- Convulsions
- Haemorrhaging under the skin

*Cause:*

The cause of red leg is due to several bacteria that are gram negative. It can be caused by Aeromonas, Proteus, E.coli and Pseudomonas bacteria.

Generally, the bacteria become present in the tank through poor husbandry of the tank. This means that the axolotl is in a tank with poor water quality caused by overcrowding, improper cleaning or overfeeding.

*Treatment:*

Treatment of red leg should be done as soon as you see red pigmentation under the skin. If you wait for the other symptoms to occur, you could run the risk of your axolotl dying.

With treatment, it is important to quarantine your axolotl, as it can be transmitted to other animals in the tank. The tank itself should be cleaned thoroughly with new water added to the tank.

Antibiotics should be administered to the axolotl. The best type of antibiotic is given through an injection; however, injections should be administered by a trained professional to prevent injuring your axolotl.

In addition, you can treat your water with 100% Holtfreter's solution. Follow the directions on the bottle. Keep your axolotl in quarantine until all symptoms of the bacteria are gone.

## *f) Columnaris*

Columnaris is another form of bacterial infection that is quite common in axolotls. Again, it can be a deadly bacteria if it is not caught quickly and treated immediately.

### *Symptoms:*

Symptoms of columnaris can often be confused with a fungus known as Saprolegnia, which is not as harmful to axolotls. However, it is important to watch for signs of distress, as this condition can be fatal for your axolotl. Symptoms include:

- Loss of appetite
- Lethargy
- Patches on the body that are white or grey

### *Cause:*

Columnaris is caused by the bacteria Chondrococcus columnaris. Again, it is often caused by poor husbandry. This means that the axolotl is in a tank with poor water quality caused by overcrowding, improper cleaning or overfeeding.

### *Treatment:*

Cleaning the tank is one of the first steps to treating columnaris, so make sure that you do a water change on the tank. In addition, add in a higher than normal dose of 100% Holtfreter's Solution into the water.

With the animal itself, fill a tub with a salt water solution. Use the same salinity as seawater; usually 2 to 3 teaspoons of salt for every litre of water. Place the axolotl in the water and allow it to sit for 5 to 10 minutes. Do not leave for longer than 10 minutes, as salt is damaging to the axolotls skin and gills so you could end up doing more harm than good.

Give the salt bath treatment once per day until the symptoms disappear.

### *g) Nitrite Poisoning*

Nitrite poisoning is a disease that occurs when there is a high level of nitrites in the tank. It is a disease that attacks the haemoglobin, which are the red pigment in your axolotl's blood. This transformation takes a blood cell that transfers oxygen through the body and turns it into a methaemoglobin, which cannot transfer blood.

### *Symptoms:*

The symptoms of nitrite poisoning are very serious and the condition can be fatal. Symptoms include:

- Gasping
- Increased gill movement
- Increased agitation

### *Cause:*

Nitrite poisoning is caused by high levels of nitrite in the tank. This is usually caused by overcrowding, overfeeding and even irregular water changes.

It can also be caused by poor maintenance of the tank.

### Treatment:
Treatment for nitrite poisoning is in correcting the nitrite levels in your tank. Make sure that you remove your axolotl to a properly cycling tank with low nitrite and ammonia levels.

While it is in the other tank, remove 20% of the water and replace it with water that is free of chlorine. In addition, clean the tank and remove any uneaten food, rotting plants or anything else that will produce a lot of ammonia, which also indicates a high level of nitrites.

### h) Ammonia Poisoning
Ammonia poisoning is a very common problem that anyone who owns an aquarium has faced at least once in their life. It is caused by the very animals that you place in the tank. Generally, what happens is that the axolotl produces too much ammonia and the bacteria in the tank is unable to eat it fast enough.

Ammonia poisoning can be prevented by adding axolotl to the tank gradually and also by having a properly cycled tank. If you do both of these things, along with keeping your tank clean, you shouldn't have any problems with ammonia.

### Symptoms:

Symptoms of ammonia poisoning range in severity as some animals tend to be hardy and able to live with the high ammonia levels longer without showing any symptoms. Symptoms include:

- Rapid breathing
- Appearance of gasping for air

- Shifts in pigmentation
- Bleeding gills

## Cause:

Ammonia poisoning is caused by high levels of ammonia in the tank. This is usually caused by overcrowding, overfeeding and even irregular water changes.

It can also be caused by poor maintenance of the tank. Finally, tanks with live plants will often see increased ammonia, as the plant life will decay naturally and release ammonia into the aquarium.

## Treatment:

Treatment for ammonia poisoning is in correcting the ammonia levels in your tank. There is nothing that you can do for the individual axolotl and hopefully, with proper cleaning of the tank, your axolotl's health will correct itself.

With treatment, remove 20% of the water and replace it with water that is free of chlorine. In addition, clean the tank and remove any uneaten food, rotting plants or anything else that will produce a lot of ammonia.

## I) Saprolegnia

Saprolegnia is a form of fungus that is commonly found in water. It can be a hassle to deal with and will affect your axolotl in a number of ways. In many cases, it is not fatal; however, if left untreated, it can become fatal.

## Symptoms:

Symptoms of Saprolegnia are very similar to those of Columnaris and the two are often mistaken for the other. Symptoms include:

- Loss of appetite
- Lethargy
- Patches on the body that are white or grey
- Open sores

One thing I want to mention is that fungus can spread over the eggs in a tank and kill the young axolotl before they even hatch. If you have fungus in your nursery aquarium, remove as many of the eggs as you can and start a new nursery.

### Causes:

Saprolegnia is caused by fungus in the water due to poor husbandry. This means that the axolotl is in a tank with poor water quality caused by overcrowding, improper cleaning or overfeeding.

### Treatment:

Cleaning the tank is one of the first steps to treating columnaris so make sure that you do a water change on the tank.

With the animal itself, fill a tub with tap water. It is better if your tap water has chloramines in it. Place the axolotl in the water and allow it to sit for 5 to 10 minutes. Do not leave for longer than 10 minutes as tap water can be very stressing for the axolotl and can lead to further problems.

Give the tap water treatment once per day until the symptoms disappear.

### j) Parasites

There are a number of parasites that can affect your axolotl and while they are different, they are often treated in the same way. Parasites can be internal or external so it is important to really watch the symptoms of the axolotl.

### Symptoms:

Symptoms vary depending on the type of parasite that is affecting the axolotl. Symptoms can be:

- Shifts in coloration
- Excess secretion of skin mucus
- Curled tail
- Loss of appetite
- Skin lesions
- Parasite on the skin
- Rashes

### Cause:

The cause of parasites is usually from adding feeder animals into the tank that carry the parasite. When the axolotl eats the animal, it contracts the parasite itself. Choosing farmed food or dead food is much better and will lower the risk of parasites entering your tank.

In addition, quarantining an axolotl before you add it to an already established tank will help prevent your new axolotl from bringing in a parasite.

### Treatment:

Treatment of parasites is usually done by placing mercurochrome into the water. For internal parasites, treatment with metronidazole is done by gut loading the feeder animals. When you are dealing with a parasite, keep the animals under quarantine until the parasite is gone.

### k) Chlorine Poisoning

Like nitrate, nitrite and ammonia poisoning, chlorine poisoning is caused when there is a high level of chlorine in the tank water. It is actually one of the easiest illnesses to avoid, as it simply requires you to avoid using tap water that hasn't been treated with dechlorinator or using water that hasn't been aged until the chlorine is gone.

### Symptoms:

As mentioned, avoiding chlorine poisoning is very simple but you should be aware of the symptoms. Symptoms are:

- Trembling
- Shifts in colouration
- Trying to get out of the water
- Increased breathing

Chlorine poisoning can be fatal if it is left untreated.

### Cause:

As I mentioned already, chlorine poisoning is caused by having untreated tap water in the tank.

### Treatment:

Treatment of chlorine poisoning is to remove the axolotl from the offending tank and place it in a tank free of chlorine. If you do not have a secondary tank to do this, use a dechlorinator in the tank. This can be risky, as some dechlorinator can be harmful to axolotl so it is important to monitor your fish while you are treating the chlorine.

### l) Fluid Build Up

The final illness that you will commonly see in your axolotl is fluid build up. This is usually seen in a growth or tumor on the axolotl's body or limbs.

### Symptoms:

Symptoms of fluid build up are exactly what it sounds like, a tumor or growth on the body or limb of the axolotl. In many cases, the axolotl does not appear to be affected by the build up.

### Cause:

Cause can be due to different reasons and may be an indication that there is a nutritional deficiency or imbalance. Actually, fluid build up is commonly seen in Metabolic Bone Disease.

Other causes of fluid build up can be old age, heart damage or kidney problems.

### Treatment:

Treatment is usually the removal of the fluid by inserting a syringe into the growth and removing the liquid. It should be noted that only a veterinarian should administer this treatment.

If there is an underlying problem, it should be diagnosed and treated as well.

## 4. Treating Your Axolotl

Treatments of disease will vary depending on the type of disease that your axolotl has. Often, treatment can be as simple as fixing the levels in your water, however, other times, an antibiotic needs to be given to the axolotl through an injection.

While I have mentioned treatment in each of the diseases that I have outlined, I did want to look at treatments in general. Many axolotl owners make the mistake of treating their axolotl with chemicals used on fish.

Although these chemicals are safe for fish, they are actually quite harmful to axolotl. They can lead to some illnesses and in some cases; they can lead to the death of the axolotl. For this reason, do not use any chemicals that are recommended for fish.

In addition, try to use chemicals that are recommended for amphibians only. Remember, you want to keep your axolotl healthy and not risk future illnesses because you used the wrong products.

Some products that you should avoid are:

*- Sterazin:* This is a product that contains a high level of toxins for both fish and axolotl. Using this product can lead to poisoning of your axolotl.

*- Clout:* This product contains many of the same toxins that are found in Sterazin. Many of them are known carcinogens.

*- Protozin:* The ingredients list is not readily available for this product but it has been linked to the death of several amphibians, so I recommend not using it for this reason.

*- Cuprazin:* Again, it is filled with toxins, including copper sulphate, which is very harmful to your axolotl.

- **Rid Rot:** Finally, rid rot is a popular product and many axolotl enthusiasts have used it without any ill side effects. That being said, there are many indicators that it could lead to long-term health problems in your axolotl, so I recommend not using it.

Now that you are aware of the chemicals that you should avoid when you are caring for your axolotl, I wanted to give you a few chemicals that you can use safely when you are treating the water or an illness.

- **Furan-2:** This chemical is used to treat bacteria in the water or in your axolotl. It is highly effective and it is safe for your axolotl with no side effects.

- **Panacur:** Another effective chemical, it is used to treat internal parasites that your axolotl could have. It should only be given in low dosages and only when needed. Never use it if you have not seen a symptom of a parasite.

- **Metronidazole:** Another chemical used to treat parasites; it is actually an excellent treatment for food, before you give the food to your axolotl. Treat your food with the chemical and they should be parasite free by the time you feed them to your pet. You can also use it as a parasite treatment for your axolotl but again, you want to use a low dosage.

- **Melafix:** Finally, melafix is a chemical that is very effective when you are using it to treat open, external sores. Dosage should be kept low but it is usually safe for axolotls with very few side effects.

Before you try any new chemical, make sure you research the treatment to make sure that other axolotl users haven't had issues with the treatment.

## 5. Giving Injections

The final thing that I want to go over in this chapter on health is how to give an injection to your axolotl. This is something I do not recommend for the beginner, however, I would like to go over it briefly so you know how to give it.

Remember that it is best to use gloves whenever you handle your axolotl as their skin can be damaged very easily.

Once you have the axolotl, remove it from the water. It is better if you have an assistant who can hold the amphibian while you administer the injection.

Take the syringe and fill it with the medication according to the recommendation given. Remove all of the air from the medication. This is very important, as you do not want to inject air into the animal.

Locate the muscle ridge on the axolotl.

Just above the hind leg, about a millimetre in front of it and a millimetre down from the muscle ridge, you will want to inject the tip of the syringe. Do not put the entire needle in, as that is too long for an axolotl.

Plunge smoothly and quickly and then remove from the axolotl. Monitor the axolotl in his aquarium to make sure there are no adverse reactions.

One of the main reasons why I recommend having a veterinarian give the injections is because the injection should be given right between the kidney and bladder. Misjudging the spot to give the injection could cause serious, if not fatal, damage to your axolotl.

# *Chapter 10. Breeding your Axolotl*

Now that you know as much as you can about Axolotl, you may be at a place in your aquarium where you want to breed your Axolotl. This is actually a very exciting time and something that can be very rewarding if you approach it properly.

That being said, there is a lot that you should know before you begin breeding your Axolotl and in this chapter, I will go over everything that you need to know about the genetics of breeding and the mechanics of breeding and raising your Axolotl.

## *1. Genetics and Color Inheritance*

I find that one of the most interesting parts of breeding Axolotl is in the genetics. There is actually a lot of knowledge in Axolotl genetics and this should enable you to do more than simply breed two together. You can breed them to pull out certain traits, specifically when it comes to color.

With breeding, it is important to understand that axolotl have 28 chromosomes. 14 of those chromosomes come from the male and 14 come from the female. However, with axolotl, there can be a shift in the number of chromosomes that are inherited. For instance, an axolotl may inherit a random allotment of chromosomes from the grandparents of the young. For instance, if the male gives 14 chromosomes, he could give a random allotment of chromosomes from his parents. This could

104

result in the young receiving 10 paternal chromosomes along with 4 maternal chromosomes in the 14 chromosome from the father.

While this may not seem like a big deal, it provides a very unique blend of chromosomes to make every axolotl in a bunch unique and completely different from each other.

When we look at genetics and color inheritance, it can become a bit confusing. However, if you break it down to the basics, it is actually quite simple.

With color, we are looking at the pigment cells. These are known as chromatophores and there are three different types of cell that you can have in an axolotl. These are:

- *Melanophores:* These are the cells that result in the black-brown color pigment.

- *Iridophores:* The cells that produce the shiny iridescent color pigment.

- *Xanthophores:* The cells that produce two colors, yellow and red color pigments.

When it comes to the color pigments, there are actually two genes or two chromosomes that lead to the color that you are going to see in your axolotl. These are either two dominant genes, recessive genes or a combination of both. The actual genes that are inherited will produce the pigment.

In axolotl, the albino gene is actually a recessive gene that is known as "a". Some axolotl will carry the gene for albinoism without being an albino, so it is important to look at both the parents of your axolotl and the breeding axolotl to help determine the colors that you are going to get.

105

When we break down color inheritance in axolotl, we look at it in the following manner:

- Dark coloring is a dominant gene. We represent it as D in the color inheritance chart below.

- Melano coloring is usually similar to dark, also known as wild types, with less yellow in the coloring. In addition, they have a shiny ring around the eye but their coloring is lacking iridescence. It is represented with a recessive m in the chart below.

- Albino as mentioned, is represented by a recessive a.

With coloring, if you breed two axolotl together that are both D/D, dark, wild coloring, then you will only produce offspring that have the same coloring. It is when you breed mixed parents that you begin to see some shifts in the coloring.

Color variants are described as the following:

| Gene | Coloring | Gene | Coloring | Gene | Coloring |
|------|----------|------|-----------|------|-----------|
| D/D | Dark | M/M | No Effect | A/A | No Effect |
| D/d | Dark | M/m | No Effect | A/a | No Effect |
| d/d | White | m/m | Melano | a/a | Albino |

So while this may seem confusing, when you breed an a/a or albino with a D/D, which is a dark, you will produce offspring that are golden albino. The lack of melanophores in the skin, combined with normal pigment creates a combination where only the yellow pigments show in the colouring.

If you are just starting in the world of axolotl breeding, then colour inheritance is not something that you will be concerned with. However, as you begin to learn about your axolotl, you will begin to pick and choose your breeding axolotl with colour inheritance in mind.

## 2. Choosing your Breeding Axolotl

Although color inheritance will play an important part in choosing your breeding axolotl, there is a bit more that you should know about your axolotl before you choose.

First, it is important to remember that axolotl should never be breed until they are full size. This is very important for the female, since breeding puts more strain on the female than the male.

Second, you should only breed after your axolotl has reached the age of 18 months. By waiting, you won't shorten the lifespan of your axolotl by putting unnecessary strain on them.

When it comes to sexual maturity, axolotl mature at different rates. In fact, many can reach sexual maturity by as young as 5 months of age, while others can take over 2 years to reach it. The main reason why there is such a fluctuation on sexual maturity in axolotl is because their growth is affected by several factors including:

- Water Temperature

- Water Conditions

- Food Quality

- Frequency of Feeding

With selections, you want to make sure that your axolotl is at least 10 inches in length; however, it is better for the female if you wait until she is her full size of 12 inches.

The main reason why you should wait for the female to mature completely is because a female axolotl will produce upwards of 1000 eggs each time she is bred.

Once she has laid her eggs, her body will begin to produce a new batch of eggs and this can take a lot out of the female, which can hinder her overall health and growth.

When you are determining if your axolotl has reached sexual maturity, you want to look for the following traits.

- *Size:* They should be at least 7 inches in length for males and 10 inches in length for females.

- *Rounded Body:* This only applies to females as the rounded bodies are due to the presence of eggs.

- *Dirty Feet:* In albino, golden and white axolotls, the tips of the toes will look "dirty" due to a darkening of the toes. There should be a dark brown tip to the toes.

- *Pale Feet:* Melanoid and wild type axolotls will have the reverse from the albino when they reach sexual maturity. In these color variations, the toes will begin to lighten, although they will still maintain a dark coloration.

While they are very slight traits to look for, it is important to choose breeding axolotls that have these traits. If they are missing one or two of the traits, do not breed them.

## 1. Mating

Once you have selected your axolotls for breeding, it is time to let mating occur. One thing that I want to mention about mating is that male axolotls go through periods when they are not producing sperm. This is a random occurrence so there will be times when you place a male into an enclosure with a female and there will be no result.

While mating can occur at any time of the year, many breeders find that they have the most success when breeding is initiated from December to June.

Breeding is actually quite simple and when you break it down, it is usually just placing a male and female together. However, there are steps that you will need to take to help initiate a "season" in your axolotls.

Again, this is debated by breeders but most agree that having a shift in temperature and light will cause the axolotls to become active for breeding. To do this, expose your axolotls to a decrease in daylight for 2 to 3 weeks. Once they have had that decrease, begin to increase the amount of light they get in a day. This should be a gradual increase and not rushed and will usually take a few weeks.

The decrease and increase of light will create a false shift in seasons and often, this will cause the axolotls to begin courtship.

Another step that may be used to initiate courtship is to change the temperature of the water. Again, this should be a gradual shift and should be done in separate tanks, not in the actual breeding tank.

Place the male and female axolotl in separate aquariums that have a water temperature of 20 to 22°C or 68 to 71°F for several weeks. After the time is up, place them into a tank together where the water is at least 5°C cooler. Usually, you want the water to be between 12 to 14°C or 54 to 57°F. When they are placed in the cooler water, after having been in the warm temperature, courtship is initiated.

It is important to note that axolotls that are kept in a room with some seasonal change, such as more or less light, are more likely to breed naturally, without the need for a temperature shift in the water.

However, when you allow them to breed naturally, you won't be as sure of when you will be producing hatchlings.

### a) The Tank

Besides the temperature and light in the breeding tank, it is important to have a proper set up for the tank. Generally, you should have a large number of plants in the tank, which is important for the spawning, as the female will lay her eggs on the plants. While you can use live, it is easier for maintaining the tank if you use plastic plants. In addition, you will want to have flat rocks and stones on the bottom of the tank for the males to deposit their spermatophores, which is the cap of sperm that the female will pick up for fertilization.

Placement of the tank is also important, as you want to put it away from windows or where it will receive a shift in temperature. In addition, you want it to be out of the way so the axolotl are not disturbed while they are mating. If they are disturbed, the courtship may not be successful.

### b) Courtship

As I have mentioned already, when the axolotl are in season and ready for breeding, they will initiate a courtship when they are placed in the tank together.

The courtship lasts from a few hours to two days; however, every pair is different. What will be the same is the courtship dance.

When the two are placed in the tank, the male should begin to swim around the tank, raising its tail in the water and writhing vigorously. The female will usually swim around the tank in a normal manner but she will occasionally nudge the male's vent.

In addition, the male will touch the female's vent during the courtship and he will lead her around the tank. As the courtship progresses, the male will begin leaving spermatophore, which is a packet of sperm attached to jelly, around the tank.

The number of spermatophore varies from male to male but you should see a minimum of 5, with some males depositing up to 25 spermatophores in a courtship.

Once the spermatophores are deposited, the male will lead the female over the spermatophore where the female will pick up one or several spermatophores and brings it into her cloaca. This allows the eggs to be fertilized inside the body of the axolotl.

### c) Spawning

After the courtship has taken place and fertilization occurs, the female axolotl will begin laying her eggs. This can occur anywhere from 2 hours after courtship to two days so don't worry if you don't see anything for the first day.

When she begins laying the eggs, she will usually lay them on the rocks and plants, which is why it is important to have those in the tank. She will lay each egg individually.

Female axolotls will lay between 100 and 1000 eggs during one spawning. Again, this varies depending on the age of the female and her health. If she is ill or is still young, she will lay fewer eggs.

### d) After Spawning

The time between courtship and spawning is very short so it is important to keep an eye on your axolotl to be aware of when the spawning has finished. Remember, don't get too close as you could affect the courtship but check occasionally to be sure that the adults are not left with the eggs for too long.

111

Once the spawning has finished, it is important to take the male and female out of the tank and place them back into their normal habitats.

Do not, and I stress this, put the female in with another male for at least a month, if not longer. While some females will produce more than one batch of eggs immediately after each other, it is not good for them to.

In fact, it is not unusual for a female axolotl to become slightly ill after breeding and should not be bred immediately again, as it can lead to serious problems for the axolotl.

## 2. The Eggs

As I have mentioned, when a female axolotl lays her eggs, she does so in the breeding tank, which will become your hatching tank. She will lay up to 1000 eggs in one breeding.

One thing that is important to note is that axolotl are not a mothering species. Like many amphibians, they will lay their eggs and leave their young to grow on their own. For this reason, be sure to take both the male and female out of the tank as soon as the eggs are hatched.

Axolotl eggs take between 2 to 3 weeks to hatch and again, this can vary depending on the water quality and temperature. With the hatchery, you want to make sure that the eggs are kept in a tank that has a steady temperature of 20°C or 68°F.

In addition, the tank should have an air pump and air stone to help keep the water aerated. Do not create a heavy current with your air pump but turn it on high enough where you get a good aeration through the water. If you fail to have good aeration, your eggs will die before the hatchlings can hatch.

The eggs range in color depending on the color of the female, so don't be surprised if you have different colored eggs with each female you have.

The development of the eggs is very interesting and you can actually see the axolotls developing in the eggs over the 3 weeks that they are growing.

When we look at the development, you will see the following, which will help you determine if the eggs were fertilized.

- **Day One:** The eggs are laid on the plants and stones in the tank. They are usually a white egg surrounded by a clear jelly.

- **Day Two:** The eggs still look the same; however, you may see bubbles sticking to the jelly. This is completely normal so don't panic if you see it.

- **Day Three:** Although the difference is very small, the embryo in the middle of the jelly has flattened slightly. This is one of the first signs that the egg has been fertilized.

- **Day Four:** You should be able to clearly differentiate between the fertilized eggs and the unfertilized eggs by day four. During this day, the fertilized eggs should begin to become an oblong shape taking up less than half of the clear jelly sphere.

- **Day Five:** By day five, you should be able to see the shape of the axolotl beginning. At this time, there should be a tail bud shape emerging from your axolotl embryos. They should still be in the protective clear jelly.

*- Day Six:* The tail bud of the embryo is well defined by this point and the external gills should be developing. In fact, you should be able to see the buds of the gills.

*- Day Seven:* There is not a lot of change between day six and day seven, however, if you use a magnifying glass, you should be able to see the start of pigment on your axolotl embryos.

*- Day Eight:* The head of the embryo is beginning to take shape on day 8 and the gills can be clearly seen. Again, the embryos are still safe inside their sphere of jelly.

*- Day Ten:* During the last few days, you should see some rotation and movement of the embryo. In addition, the heart and liver is developed, which is seen as a colored spot on the ventral side of each embryo.

*- Day Twelve:* The eyes of the embryo have developed and if there are any pigments, you should be able to see it quite clearly by this day.

*- Day Thirteen:* By day thirteen, your embryos should begin to hatch, although they will not be swimming around your tank. Instead, they will hatch within the jelly and will begin to eat the yolk. This is a very important stage and the embryos, known as larvae at this stage, need the nourishment from the yolk.

*- Day Fourteen and on:* From day 14 and onwards, the larvae will break free of their jelly and be fully hatched. This is when they will begin swimming freely around the tank and it will be a very exciting time for you.

While the egg stage can seem like a boring stage of your breeding tank, it is actually one that is quite interesting and full of things for you to see.

## *3. The Hatchlings*

Now that your larvae have hatched, it is time to care for them. At this point, there isn't a lot that you have to do, simply provide them with a proper hatchery, which you did earlier.

Remember to keep the water properly maintained. If you are unsure of how to maintain it, please read the chapter on your tank set up. In addition, keep the water temperatures and the aeration at the same level as you did when you had eggs.

The hatchlings are very self sufficient and will usually grow at their own speed. It can usually take about 3 weeks before they are considered to be juvenile axolotls.

The hatchlings are usually about 11mm in length when they hatch. When they do hatch, they do not have any front or back legs and look very similar to a tadpole.

Within the first week, their legs will develop; however, they usually develop their front legs around the time they are 20 mm in length and their back legs when they are about 1.5cm in length.

It is very important during this time that you really watch your larvae. While you can hatch hundreds of larvae, the rate of death can be surprisingly high if you are not careful.

First, axolotl larvae are delicate and can be affected by poor water quality and lack of food. In addition, they are known to be cannibalistic and will consume each other. The best way to avoid this is to keep several tanks.

As they are growing, remove the largest axolotl larvae and place them in a different tank. Keep them separated according to size so they are less likely to prey on smaller larvae. In addition, keeping a lot of plants in the tank will give the larvae places to hide from their larger siblings.

Another reason for the mortality rate in axolotl larvae is genetic malformations. This will lead to the larvae dying off. Again, when they die, the other larvae will consume them, however, you can remove them from the tank to prevent that.

### a) Feeding your Hatchlings

Feeding your larvae can be difficult if you are not prepared for it. Remember, they are very small and most of the hatchlings will be no larger than 13mm in length. That means that the food they eat is very limited and needs to be small as well.

With newly hatched axolotl, it is important to feed them small food within 24 hours of hatching. If they aren't fed properly, they can suffer greatly in their health and could die. In addition, axolotl larvae should be fed two or three times a day, gradually decreasing the frequency as they get older.

Since they are hunters, axolotl larvae need to be fed live food. The best choice for new hatchlings are brineshrimp. Some breeders will recommend microworms; however, they are not a good choice as they tend to be a bit too big for them when they are first hatched.

When your hatchlings grow in size, you can begin introducing larger food for them to eat, including the microworms, which are high in nutritional value for axolotls.

Food that you can give your hatchlings are:

- ***Brineshrimp:*** Also known as Artemis shrimp or BBS, you should choose brineshrimp that is actually freshly hatched when you have young larvae. What this means is that you should get a package of brineshrimp eggs and hatch them in a separate tank. As soon as they are hatched, use a very small kitchen strainer lined with nylons and strain them out of the brineshrimp hatchery.

Rinse them off with fresh water to remove the salt and place them into the tank with the hatchlings. The hatchlings will eat these readily.

As your hatchlings grow, they will begin to eat the adult brineshrimp but while they are young, they should only eat the brineshrimp babies.

*- Water Fleas:* Also known as Daphnia or moina, these are excellent food for new axolotl hatchlings. They need to be hatched in the same manner as brineshrimp, in a separate tank, but they are a bit more difficult to hatch and take about 2 weeks to do so.

*- Blackworms:* Blackworms are recommended for your larvae when they are older and not when they are still young due to their size. Juvenile axolotl can eat whole blackworms and the larvae themselves can eat chopped up pieces of blackworm. One of the biggest benefits of blackworms is that they will continue to wriggle for several days after they have been chopped up, this means the predatory axolotl larvae will eat them.

Another benefit is that they are very nutritious for axolotl and they can be found at most pet stores, making them easy to obtain and sustain.

*- Whiteworms:* Another worm that is good for young axolotl larvae are whiteworms. They can be purchased in a variety of sizes, making them easy to use, as you can purchase according to the size of your axolotl.

One thing that should be mentioned with whiteworms is that these should not be the main source of food for your axolotl. Although it is not conclusive, there have been some links to lack of pigment development in your axolotl when their primary diet is white worms.

*- Tubifex Worms:* Tubifex worms come in a variety of sizes and are another food that is excellent for axolotl larvae. They are full of nutrition for axolotl; however, they can be difficult to find if you are not set up to culture them yourself. Usually, you will need to purchase them from an aquarist and not an actual pet store.

*- Bloodworms:* Although they are not that good for young larvae, they can be very good for juvenile axolotl, as they are full of nutrition. One of the downsides of bloodworms is that they are usually very messy.

*- Pellets:* The final food that you can feed your axolotl larvae is pellets. This is only recommended for axolotl larvae that are larger than 2 cm. Smaller axolotl cannot swallow the pellets and will usually ignore them because they are not alive. Most pet stores sell pellets for axolotls, newts and other salamanders.

### b) Juvenile Axolotl

By the time your axolotl larvae have grown their front legs and their hind legs are developing, they are a juvenile. This is an exciting time as you can move them into their permanent enclosures at this time, although I recommend that you wait until their back legs are fully grown.

Once they are a juvenile, you can begin feeding them pellets and you can also feed them small pieces of earthworm. At this time, the growth that had been quite rapid before now slows down significantly. In fact, you should expect a slow, steady growth during this time.

And that is everything that you need to know concerning breeding your axolotl and caring for their young.

# *Chapter 11. Common Terms*

So you are interested in owning a Mexican Salamander; well if you want to be a true Mexican Salamander lover and owner, it is important to understand a few of the common terms that you will hear the moment you enter the Mexican Salamander raising world. Below is a list of terms and words that you will experience.

*- Ambystoma:* The axolotl's cup like mouth.

*- Ammonia:* A gaseous compound that is found in the decaying plant life of an aquarium and also in the waste of the axolotl.

*- Amphibian:* A cold blooded vertebrate that starts its life in water with gills and develops until it has grown legs and the ability to breathe air. The animal is semiterresterial.

*- Aquarist:* A person who owns and manages a home aquarium.

*- Aquarium:* A tank or bowl that is made of glass where aquatic animals are kept in water.

*- Buccal Respiration:* The act of breathing through the Buccopharyngeal Membrane.

*- Buccopharyngeal Membrane:* A flap of skin that is found near the back of the throat in the axolotl.

*- Capillaries:* Small blood vessels. Primarily used to describe parts of the gills in the axolotl.

*- Carnivore:* An animal that eats meat as its primary food source.

*- Cloacal:* The cavity on an amphibian that houses the reproductive organs, intestinal tract and urinary tract.

- *Cutaneous Respiration:* The act of breathing through the skin. This occurs when oxygen enters the body through the thin layer of skin.

- *Fimbrea:* The capillaries found in the gills.

- *Gills:* The organ found on the sides of the axolotl in large fluffy branches that enable the axolotl to breathe under water.

- *Hatchling:* The young axolotl immediately after it has been hatched.

- *Herbivore:* An animal that primarily eats vegetation and plants as its main food source.

- *Iridophores:* Shiny patches on the body and around the eyes of an axolotl.

- *Juvenile:* A young axolotl that has developed all of its limbs but has not reached sexual maturity.

- *Larva:* The stage of development in the axolotl's lifecycle where the axolotl does not have any legs.

- *Melanophores:* These are the cells that result in the black-brown color pigment.

- *Neoteny:* Also known as pedogenesis, it refers to an animal that retains its juvenile or larval form throughout its life, even after sexual maturity.

- *Omnivore:* An animal that eats both plants and meat.

- *Pedicalate:* A mouth that is used for holding food and not for cutting and biting

- *Poikilothermic:* Refers to an animal that is cold blooded.

- *Rami:* The gills of the axolotl.

- *Regeneration:* The growth of new cells after an injury.

- *Spermatophores:* A capsule of sperm that the male axolotl lays in the aquarium.

- *Substrate:* The base materials that are placed on the floor of the aquarium.

- *Vent:* An opening on the underside of the axolotl that contains the sexual organs.

- *Xanthophores:* The cells that produce two colors, yellow and red color pigments.